HOW TO HUNT
NORTH AMERICAN
BIG GAME

By C. E. HAGIE

THE MACMILLAN COMPANY · NEW YORK

1946

Dedication

This volume is affectionately dedicated to my wife Ruby, who, as a bride, accompanied me to a mountain ranch on the Montana frontier forty miles from the nearest town, who did her full share of the drudgery on a cattle ranch without complaint, who reared a family, hunted with me, camped with me, and finally assumed the whole responsibility of typing and putting in shape the manuscripts for this and my book *The American Rifle*—the best cook in the West, a good rifle shot, a loyal companion, and a charming hostess.

C. E. HAGIE

Foreword

FOLLOWING World War I there was an almost immediate increase of 20 per cent in the number of persons participating in hunting activities in the United States. The mounting interest could be accounted for as a result of two distinct causes: first, several million young men who returned from military camps and battlefields where they had been accustomed to the use of firearms, were prepared to turn to hunting as a civilian recreation; second, the strain imposed by the war years resulted in psychological tensions and shattered nerves which caused thousands who had never before done so to seek the relaxing effects of outdoor recreation, and many adopted hunting as a major hobby.

Government statistics indicate that of the first draft of boys for World War II, only 2 per cent had ever shot a gun of any kind before entering military camp. At least three times as many Americans have been trained in the use of firearms in World War II as in World War I, and the nervous strain on the country as a whole has been much more intense. Wildlife specialists believe that the increased interest in hunting upon the return of the boys in service will boost the immediate post-war national increase to 30 per cent or 40 per cent above the pre-war period. It is fortunate that the country's big game populations have more than trebled since the close of the previous world war, so that the country is prepared to take care of the increased numbers of prospective hunters.

In the belief that such a volume as this will fill a real need on the part of the rising generation of sportsmen who will take up the hunting of North America's big game animals as a relaxation from the perplexities of the post-war years, this guide to big game hunting has been prepared. It has been designed as an authentic and reliable source of information on most of the questions concerning how to hunt North America's big game animals, from selecting the hunting territory to bringing home and caring for the meat and trophies.

The author writes from more than thirty years' experience in big game hunting, from New Mexico to Alaska and from the Pacific coast to the north woods. Ten years were spent as a rancher in one of the finest big game districts of Montana, two years in Alaska, seven years in the north woods country, eight years in Colorado's best game district, with experience as a guide and packer, two listings in *Records of North American Big Game*, authorship of the companion book *The American Rifle for Hunting and Target Use*, and for the past four years all the wildlife photography in connection with building up the Colorado Game and Fish Department's film library. Except as otherwise indicated, photographs are by the author.

It is my sincere hope that the information and advice contained in this handbook may mean the difference between disappointment and success on that big game hunting trip, besides being the means of saving thousands of tons of game meat that might otherwise spoil as a result of improper handling; and that the readers' trophies may arrive at the tanneries and the taxidermist shops in fit condition to be a lasting pride instead of a cause for embarrassment. Its reading is commended to the seasoned hunter as well as to the one preparing for his first big game hunt.

C. E. HAGIE

Contents

Illustrations

Acknowledgments

The author wishes to give due credit for the photographs listed below:

CHAPTER I

Selection of a Hunting Country

THE most important thing in connection with planning a hunting trip is the selection of the country to be hunted. This is just as true of the farmer or rancher in the heart of the hunting country as of the sportsman 2,000 miles away who lays his plans months in advance of the trip. The only difference is in the degree and scope of planning to be done. In the first instance, the local resident has first-hand access to all the facts. He probably knows by past experience where his game is accustomed to feed and water, and in what patch of timber or creek bottom or clump of brush or rocky bench it is likely to be spending its resting time at the particular season of the year. If he doesn't know these things, it will be wise for him to make a pre-season survey of the surrounding country to find where the freshest signs are and to avoid spending his first half day or day of hunting in a sterile area.

Many factors may change the population concentration from year to year. To mention but a few, the grazing of domestic sheep over a particular range is likely to discourage its use by such animals as deer and elk for a considerable length of time. Overbrowsing either by too much game during a preceding winter or by domestic livestock will cause a movement to better feed. Springs may go dry, salt put out for domestic stock may be distributed differently than during the preceding year, a dog in the neighborhood may have developed game-chasing tendencies, the leaves may have gone from the trees earlier than usual, the acorn crop of the area may have failed—in fact, a hundred things may have happened to cause a local shift in game populations.

As I write this, an aerial survey of deer populations in Colorado shows a shift of several thousand from one mountain slope to another as compared with exactly a year ago. Why? Possibly a difference in snowfall between the two

A typical hunting lodge in the western mountains.

winters; possibly a difference in feed conditions; possibly a combination of the two, or even some other factors we have not given consideration. The point is that the man who plans a hunting trip should know in advance where he is likely to find plenty of the animals he plans to hunt.

The farther the sportsman is from the hunting territory, the more complicated and complex are the problems involved in selecting his place to hunt. The Denver sportsman, as an example, may know that he will certainly hunt in Colorado. His first problem is to decide which one of many counties or which one of many river drainages or plateaus is likely to afford the best opportunity to bag his game in the shortest time or with the least effort, or where the largest heads are likely to be found, or where the game is most accessible to where he can drive his automobile. The location of friends with whom he can stay or who will assist him in determining the exact whereabouts of the game, may be a deciding factor. To say the least, the latter consideration is very important.

The man who lives far away in some state that has no big game, will first have to decide the state in which he expects to hunt. After he does this, his problems are still very much more difficult than those of the man whom we considered above, because he is far removed from his source of direct information. He isn't likely to have a neighbor who hunts regularly and who can get him in on a party already organized, or tip him off on the best place to go. He must start gathering this information from scratch. He may write to guides advertising in the sportsmen's magazines, but a lot of these are not in the best hunting country. He may write to the State Game Department of the state he has chosen, but sometimes they have little information of a specific nature to make available.

Some states like Colorado and California have made detailed studies of where game was killed the previous year, and can supply it in map form. From such a map one can get a very authentic picture of where successful hunters are finding their game. The areas of heaviest kill may not always be the places of heaviest concentration of animals, but they are likely to indicate the districts where hunters' chances of success are greatest. Often the areas of heaviest game concentration are remote from roads, and sometimes they embrace terrain and cover where successful hunting is very difficult. To cite an example of this type: I rode three days in a district of extremely heavy elk concentration where fresh tracks were

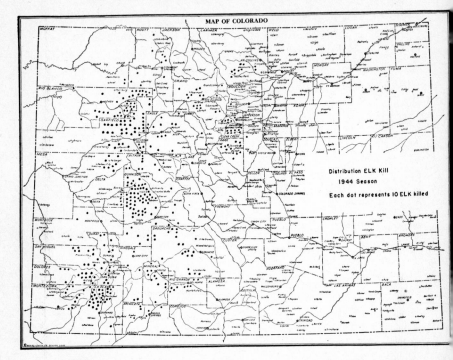

everywhere in evidence, without seeing an elk. The animals were in very heavy timber where they could hear the hunter many times as far away as he could glimpse them. I have frequently hunted deer and bear under similar circumstances. It should be obvious that areas of consistently heavy hunter-kills of game are safer choices for the hunter than mere localities of heavy concentrations of animals. A map of the type indicated is appended in order that the reader may more readily visualize its significance in connection with choosing an area in which to hunt.

Another major aid to prospective hunters that may be secured from the State Game Department of many of the more important big game states, is a list of guides and those catering to the convenience and comfort of the sportsman. By corre-

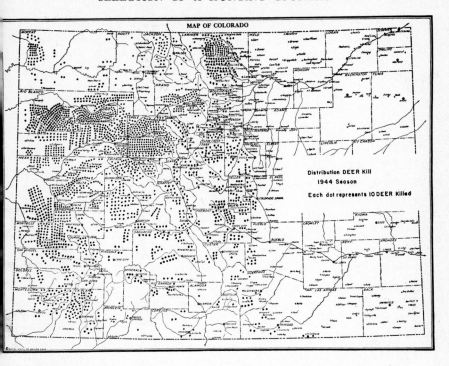

MAP OF COLORADO

Distribution DEER Kill
1944 Season

Each dot represents 10 DEER Killed

sponding with someone on such a list, located in or near the district chosen for the hunt, even the inexperienced hunter should be able to line himself up for a successful as well as enjoyable hunt within the range of his pocketbook. Such connections invariably make horses available for packing meat and trophies, as well as packing camp equipment in, if the hunting is to be done in the back country. It is surprising what a small fee many western ranchers place upon their services and hire for their horses and other transportation equipment. On the other hand, there are deluxe outfits that are willing to provide every luxury the sportsman is willing to pay for, and guarantee shots at game, or guarantee the game in the bag, if that is what the hunter wants (even if the guide has to shoot it).

As a suggestion to those seeking any of the services mentioned above, I would advise that the sportsman start his
negotiations well in advance of the opening of the hunting
season, because the total of all such accommodations are far
less than the total demand for them. With the return to civilian life of millions of young men from the world's fighting
fronts who will almost certainly swell the ranks of the big
game hunting fraternity, the shortage of ranch accommodations and guides in comparison with the demand will be
many times accentuated.

Another common source of information for the sportsman in states where the State Game Department does not
maintain lists of accommodations, is the State Tourist Bureau or State Publicity Bureau. Another very helpful source
of information is the Chamber of Commerce in the principal
town of the district in which the sportsman is interested. It
is almost universally true, especially in the West, that these
local civic organizations are very anxious to attract visitors
to their locality and will go out of their way to accommodate
the sincere inquirer.

One planning to hunt in Alaska or Canada will undoubtedly
be wise to secure a list of registered guides and depend upon
them for preliminary information. Most of the towns in the
hunting country maintain some type of civic club or other
organization willing to answer correspondence and provide
such advice and assistance as they may have, including the
recommendation of reliable frontiersmen in the best big game
districts.

For the adventurous ones who are more interested in having
a rugged vacation in the great outdoors than in bagging game
in a minimum amount of time or of being certain of bagging
any game at all, an automobile with a trailer, a tent, a camp
outfit, and a map will provide the hunting vacation at least
expense. Under these circumstances it may require several

years to get acquainted with a hunting country as well as one might do in a half day with a competent guide or a resident farm or ranch owner who knows every foot of the country and the habits of the game inhabiting it. The hunter who chooses to free-lance in this way should be very careful that he does not trespass on the property rights of others or violate the rules of government agencies on whose land he may camp or hunt. Many a hunting part on public land has been compelled to travel back long distances to clean up camp-sites, in order to avoid prosecution in court for violating regulations.

CHAPTER II

What to Take and Not to Take on a Hunting Trip

Most hunters take at least twice as much duffle on the hunting trip as they ever have occasion to use. For the person who has plenty of hired help and unlimited facilities for transportation in connection with every phase of his activities, it probably doesn't make much difference if he does add another cooking range and a 20 × 30-foot portable house. But for the average hunter who has to depend upon a limited number of pack-horses, and may even have to pack a lot on his own back of what he takes into camp, it is wise to leave all the unessentials at home. The question resolves itself into determining what the bare essentials are.

The rifle (or shotgun, in states where rifles are not permitted in hunting camps), a minimum amount of ammunition, a pocket-knife, and matches are the primary essentials. I have hunted many places where I didn't even carry a lunch but depended for food on the small game I could kill and roast, without salt, over a camp-fire; but this is the other extreme.

Two years ago a party of us got into good elk country in late afternoon about 10 miles from our base camp. The others considered it impossible to stay on the mountain all night above timber-line without food or shelter, and rode back to camp, returning the following morning. When they arrived next morning I was eating a breakfast of elk heart roasted over a camp-fire, and during three more days not another elk was killed from that camp. I relate this merely as proof that it is possible to get along without blankets or conventional provisions if one knows how to do it. One can be fairly comfortable even in the coldest weather under a brush lean-to with a small fire in front of it, or even with his back to a windbreak of almost any kind, and a fire in front. A blanket helps but is not necessary. I have two or three friends who hunt mountain lions and never pack either a blanket or provisions in the most severe weather, knowing that it may be a week or two before they get back to either conventional food or shelter.

For the hunter who wants at least a minimum of civilized comforts and the more valuable of the auxiliary gadgets, the following is a list in the order of their importance: sleeping-bag or two or three wool blankets, skillet, tin plate, cup, knife, fork, and spoon, salt, pair of binoculars of 6 to 8 power, sheath knife, camp ax, shovel, light tent, extra handkerchiefs, extra suit of underwear and socks, compass (for those who need one), 15 feet of heavy sash cord, cake of soap and towels. The soap will make life seem more civilized, although ordinary silt or soil will remove dirt or grease almost as well as the best of soap.

If the hunter wants to go beyond these primary conveniences, he may add two or three pans or a nested camp-kit of utensils, an extra shirt and pair of pants, a pair of light shoes for wear in camp, a small meat saw, an air mattress, an electric or gasoline lantern, a collapsible sheet-metal wood-burning stove or a gasoline camp-stove (by turning large tin or sheet-metal pans upside down over each burner, it will make a first-class heating unit for the tent), nails, a small pillow, a 7 × 9-foot tarpaulin, folding camp-chairs, a collapsible table, pajamas, toilet articles including toilet paper (better leave the shaving equipment at home for the beard will protect the face from sun, wind, and weather), a small-caliber pistol or revolver, camera, snake-bite kit (if in snake country), an alkalizer (baking soda will do the trick), small first-aid kit,

Four men on horseback comfortably outfitted for two weeks in the back country, San Juan Primitive Area, Colorado.

fishing tackle (if it is legal to fish in your hunting country), and pills if you need them.

Don't take any of the following items on a hunting trip:

hard liquor, bed-springs (boughs, grass, or twigs are better), heavy mattress, coal or heavy wood-burning stove, more than one change of clothes unless the trip is to be a month or more in length and transportation is not a major item, more than one rifle, a shotgun unless it is the primary hunting weapon, more than two pairs of shoes or boots for field use (one of leather and one of rubber), quilts (use wool blankets), golf clubs, cots or bedsteads, chairs or tables that are not collaps-ible, mirror, hair tonic, trunks, chests of drawers, framed pictures, bathtub, dogs (where their use is prohibited), poisons of any kind, your wife (unless she is one in a thousand and can really enjoy roughing it—and then don't expect her to do the cooking), anyone as a member of the party who is un-likely to carry his full share of the camp drudgery cheerfully.

As to the type of food to take on a hunting trip where you are not depending on a local host to provide it and someone to call "come and get it" at regular intervals, there are some general principles that should be strictly adhered to. The first of these is to consider the keeping qualities of foods in terms of the weather that may be anticipated on your trip, bearing in mind that a deep hole dug in the ground and cov-ered with a gunny-sack filled with grass or leaves will keep foods relatively cool in summer and warm enough in winter to prevent freezing. Bread will mold very quickly in some climates; canned goods and fruits and vegetables will freeze in others. Many foods are affected adversely by conditions of weather and temperature. Take only what you are cer-tain will not be wasted because of climatic conditions.

Bulk and weight of certain types of food are major factors in determining under what circumstances they should be taken or left at home. If there is a good road to the hunting camp and the party travels by automobile with a trailer at-tached to bring back the game, there is no reason why bulky foods should not be included. In such cases, fresh fruits, vegetables, canned goods, and even pastries can be included and the menu may follow conventional home cooking lines, if the party has one competent to do that kind of cooking; but the average hunting party can't plan on doing things this way.

If very many hunting parties camped on roads where a car

Camp diet can often be varied with fresh fish.

with a trailer could be driven, especially in the West, there would be very little game killed, for the game would move into the back country and leave the hunters out on the fringe holding an empty bag.

The most sensible principle to follow is to plan the larder so that it will occupy a minimum of space and weigh as little as possible. While canned goods are convenient to pack and to use, they usually occupy from three to five times the space, and weigh at least four times as much as the same foods in a dehydrated state. A variety of food is desirable, but not at all necessary. Extensive experiments in the arctic have demonstrated that an exclusive fresh meat diet will keep the body in good condition and health not only for months at a time

Groceries "cupboard boxes" designed for use on pack saddle without panniers. Straps fasten them directly to the saddle.

but for years; and fresh meat should be plentiful on a hunting trip. I am not recommending an exclusive meat diet, but just calling attention to facts. A variety of dried fruits and vegetables is recommended for the hunting camp. Bacon is a good staple item for almost any hunting camp at any time of year, and provides a residue of fat for other cooking purposes. Butter or margarine, sugar, salt, pepper, flour, a ready-mixed pancake flour, cheese, dehydrated eggs, coffee or tea, oatmeal, one of the highly compressed breads (of the hardtack type), baking powder, soda—these are all standard items.

Many hunters like such canned meat as Spam, which is not excessively bulky. Others insist that a few small jars of jam or jelly are almost a necessity. Don't take syrups; they can be made from plain sugar with a few drops of flavoring such as Mapleine if desired. There is no sense in packing the water on the trip. Bars of sweet chocolate provide a quick pickup; dried beef or jerked venison is good for pocket lunches, or even for the overnight stay. For those who know nothing about how much of what to take along, or how to cook it after they arrive in camp, it is better to invest in a good book on camp cookery.

For the man who hunts regularly, there is nothing like a good strong pair of panniers to fit a pack-saddle, with a light strong box fitted to each, into which the groceries, etc., can be packed. Some design these so that when removed they practically constitute a cupboard to be used as needed. They offer protection against flies, mice, rats, and other rodents. Don't take an ice-box on a hunting trip. In the arctic you can have a real ice-box even with the mercury at 80 degrees, by just chopping a hole 2 or 3 feet deep in the ground. Even in our warmest climates, a hole dug into the ground in the shade and covered over is a great help in saving foods.

CHAPTER III

How to Dress on a Hunting Trip

IMPROPER clothing has made many a man miserable on a hunting trip and has ruined the success of even more.

It should be obvious to everyone that hunting clothing should first be suited to the type of weather likely to be encountered *where* the hunting is to be done and *how* the hunting is to be done. In the South, comfort dictates light clothing, and warm weather with a high degree of humidity discourages an excessive amount of physical exercise. Perhaps this is why most southern hunting is done by driving the game past hunters standing or sitting quietly at places where the animals are most likely to pass. For such hunting, whether it is done in the South, the East, the North or West, comfort is the major factor, except that as a safety measure some bright color such as red should be worn. This will insure against being mistaken for the animal being hunted, should some other hunter come along and take a pot-shot at "something the color of a deer (or a bear) which moved in the brush," that later turned out to be *you*.

As a general principle, the man out-of-doors who expects to perspire profusely on a long hard hike uphill for an hour and stand or sit quietly in a chill wind at alternate intervals (as most hunters will certainly have plenty of occasions to do), should be dressed in wool clothing from the skin out. Perspiration-soaked underwear of cotton, linen, or silk will cling to one's body like a wet dishrag, and with even a mod-

15

erate breeze blowing will be about as comfortable as a sheet of ice next to the skin.

Woolen garments are sufficiently porous that the dead air spaces provide nearly as good insulation for the body when wet as when dry and protect it against otherwise sudden temperature changes. I make it a practice when either hunting or hiking in the mountains, to wear light, full-length, woolen underwear in summer as well as in winter. It is quite a general practice among frontier mountain men. From the standpoint of mere warmth, it is not so necessary that the outer garments be of wool; but weight for weight, wool shirts, pants, and blouses are warmer than any other material except feathers.

For wear in the most extreme cold, quilted blouses and pants of duck down are the last word in warmth. Many westerners wear pants and blouses of heavy jean or light duck the year round as the outer garments. As the weather gets colder they just add another wool shirt and an extra pair of wool trousers under the jean, which function primarily as a windbreaker. The hunter, however, has other factors to consider than just warmth and comfort.

When I first started hunting big game, I wore a pair of corduroy pants, hobnail boots, a hard-twist cotton jacket, and a stiff-brimmed hat. I couldn't understand why all the game left the vicinity before I arrived, even when I was traveling into the wind. I was telling my hard-luck story to an old-timer who had spent twenty years hunting big game for the early mining camp markets. He was not surprised. "Sure," he said, "they hear you coming."

We sat down together and I got the most valuable lecture on hunting that anyone ever listened to. It should be perfectly obvious to anyone but a tenderfoot that hobnails on rock make a lot of noises not associated with nature. I was told then, and I have proved it to be absolutely true, that big game animals are quick to recognize anything that is unlike the customary sounds of nature, and that they are immediately suspicious and on their guard. It had never occurred to me that the sound of a twig rubbing against my jacket or corduroys was radically unlike a twig brushing the side of a deer, or in fact that such a sound would even be perceived by them. In many years of experience since that time, I have verified the fact that the old market-hunter was 100 per cent correct in his conclusions.

You can scare most species of big game animals into flight long before you can see them or they can see or scent you, by the sound of a hard hat brim striking a twig, or brush rubbing against cotton clothing of almost any sort. Certainly, corduroys and hard-surfaced clothing of every kind should be left at home on the hunting trip. Rubber-soled shoes are much to be preferred to hard leather soles; and for those who would be successful still-hunters, I would heartily recommend moccasins if their feet are toughened sufficiently to get along with them.

My most successful hunting was done wearing buckskin moccasins over a pair of heavy wool socks; but the average person's feet are too tender for that. Most men can, however, wear heavy moosehide moccasins or the light-soled pacs manufactured for sportsmen's use. For the man who hunts from horseback, chaps of leather tanned with the hair on are preferable to those made of ordinary leather. Leather jackets, except the soft buckskin type, are not recommended for hunting in brushy country.

Now for the question of what constitutes the best clothing to hunt in. If wet weather necessitates the use of a slicker, don't plan to do any moving around in it; let the game stumble onto you instead. In still-hunting in rainy weather I have always preferred to wear heavy wool clothing, get soaked, and change to dry clothes when back at camp. One does not chill while exercising in wet wool clothing. For most North American big game hunting it is pretty safe to plan a wardrobe made up somewhat as follows: heavy soft wool shirts, light-weight fine wool underwear, wool socks (over light silk socks if one prefers), wool pants of the soft-finish type, all-wool jacket of mackinaw cloth (moisture-proofed), rubber-bottomed pacs with 10-inch leather tops for snow and wet weather and 10-inch-top leather-soled pacs for dry weather, lined mittens for very cold days, wool cap with visor for ordinary wear or soft felt hat and knitted cap that can be pulled well down over ears and back of neck in extreme cold (never a cap of leather), a slicker for riding in the rain.

Some states require by law that all big game hunters wear red jackets and caps. Others require that some red or other bright color be worn conspicuously. Regardless of law or no law, it is "healthy" for a person on a hunting trip where many others are also carrying firearms, to adorn himself with something that will help the wild-eyed novice from mistaking him for a deer, elk, bear, moose, sheep, goat, jackass, or some other unnamed beast. If the other fellow is color-blind, it may not be complete protection. Sometimes I think that every purchaser of a hunting license should be tested for color-blindness and required to identify the picture of a deer from that of a jersey cow, an elk from a Hereford bull, a Rocky Mountain bighorn from a merino ram, and a six-months-old colt from every species of wild game, including the cow moose. Incidentally, it is a well-established fact that most species of big game are color-blind and wouldn't know the difference between red and black or yellow and white, so don't worry about color frightening them.

CHAPTER IV

Etiquette and Law in Hunter Relationships

In spite of sportsmen's clubs, Izaak Walton Leagues, and "good neighbor" ballyhoo, the relationships between hunters and landowners grow constantly more strained in many parts of the country. This may not be quite so critical in the big game hunting field as in the realm of bird and squirrel and rabbit hunting; but it is bad enough to be serious. There are already large areas of privately owned land closed to hunting, and more landowners are moving in that direction every year. It is fortunate for the West that so large a proportion of the mountainous areas are within either the national forests or the public domain under United States Grazing Service Control.

Very frankly, my own sympathies in the controversy are with the landowner. For ten years I owned and operated a cattle ranch in one of the best big game hunting districts of Montana, and seldom did a hunting season pass without the loss of a calf or a steer or a colt, or of a number of them, as the result of carelessness on the part of hunters—men in the habit of shooting first and identifying their game afterward, men who shoot into moving brush or at a sound of running animals. If sometime the sportsman finds himself with no place to hunt, it will be the fault of the thoughtlessness and laxity and deliberate lawlessness of a few members of his own clan who should be brought into line by ostracism from respectable society. They should be denied the privilege of securing licenses until they can prove they have completely reformed.

In the United States of America the landowner controls his farm or ranch or pasture-land or timber plot so completely under the law that he can prosecute trespass of any and all kinds within his boundaries. Most states have even reinforced the Common Law with statutes declaring that it is illegal to hunt or fish upon private land without the specific consent of the owner. In spite of this, many who call themselves good sportsmen will sneak onto others' land and hunt until they are discovered and driven off. Every man who hunts should, under the circumstances, have the common decency to ask the landowner for the privilege. Most owners will cheerfully grant the request. But like the rest of us, they like to know who is on their premises and what they are doing; and if damage is done, they like to know whom to blame for it. Anyone who has any regard whatever for the Golden Rule, will assuredly never again hunt or fish on another's land without first securing permission to do so. It is the first and most important principle of etiquette in every sportsman's Bible. No true sportsman will violate this rule.

Now that we have disposed of the hunter's first obligation, we shall turn to a consideration of matters that involve his relationships with his fellow sportsman. Most of the answers to these problems involve nothing more than the application of the age-old rule of doing to the other fellow as you would have him do to you. There are places where many hunting parties may camp in close proximity without lessening the other fellow's chances of getting game; and there are places and situations where there just isn't room for more than one hunting party within a limited area.

In brushy country where deer are very plentiful, it may be a distinct advantage to have fifteen or twenty hunters working together. But in most places in the West, unless men are hunting on horseback far from camp, it might be considered a serious breach of etiquette without the consent or invitation from the party first to arrive on the scene. On public land the rule is, "First come, first served." In other words, the right to a camp-site goes to the first to appropriate it, and rights do not extend from year to year nor beyond the day a site may be vacated. There are some places in the national forests where certain areas are set aside for camping. Where this is the case, other sites should not be used except by permission of the ranger in charge of the district.

It is very poor taste for a hunter to take up a position in line with where he knows other hunters are planning a drive, in order to benefit from others' efforts at their expense. It is not unethical to profit from such a drive if a hunter should take his stand beyond the most remote area to be covered by the party making the drive.

It is not good sportsmanship to kill birds and animals as camp meat on which there is no legal open season at the time. In some areas of the West the dusky grouse has been poached on heavily by big game hunters. Their numbers are kept so low that open seasons are out of the question for the law-abiding and legitimate hunter. In other parts of the country the same situation exists in regard to the ruffed grouse; and spruce grouse have been practically exterminated over vast areas by big game hunters who killed them in violation of both law and ethical practices.

There is no law on the subject, but it is good ethics never to fire the first shot at game that a companion or another hunter sees first. If he fails to hit the animal and it starts to get away, most sportsmen consider it to be entirely ethical for other hunters to take a hand in the shooting; in this case the animal will belong to the one who fires the fatal shot. It is considered good ethics for a sportsman to shoot a wounded animal being pursued by another; but in such cases the one who assisted should not lay claim to the carcass. This is the common practice among true sportsmen.

It is decidedly bad taste, even where it is not against the law, for one hunter to shoot game for another member of his party without a specific request to do so, or unanimous agreement in advance that the hunt is to be conducted in that way. Even when such an agreement is made, it can scarcely be considered good sportsmanship, because such a blanket agreement may readily result in the killing of more game than the party is entitled to.

There have been many quarrels—some of them resulting fatally—and not a few lawsuits over the ownership of dead game. If two hunters fire at an animal at practically the same instant and both bullets strike a vital spot, it is customary either to divide the carcass or to flip a coin for possession.

Other situations are not so simple. There are local rules that are observed as ethical procedure in various localities, but they differ as from East to West and as from North to South and are not recognized by the courts. In some sections the custom is to consider game to be the property of the first hunter to draw blood. The other extreme is to consider the animal to be the property of the last hunter who fired a bullet into it while it could still stand on its feet. It is obvious that somewhere between these two extremes should lie a sound basis of rightful claim to ownership.

Courts have held that game animals are the property of the state and pass into private ownership only when they have been "reduced to possession" under legal circumstances. The stumbling-block here is the term "reduced to possession," and the courts have attempted more than once to define it. Obviously, if a man, after shooting a deer and seeing it fall, goes to it and cuts its throat or sticks it in the chest, he has reduced it to possession. The fact that someone else might come along and forcibly take it from him and lock a tag on the antlers would not alter the law's interpretation of ownership. (This has actually happened.) I know of a case where a young hunter was forced at the muzzle of a gun to give up a deer he had just killed.

In a case where one hunter wounds a deer that is later killed by another, the courts have sometimes been hard put to interpret their own phraseology. In most such cases they have held that if the first hunter had discontinued "pursuit," the carcass belonged to the second hunter, regardless of the nature of the initial wound. On the other hand, they have held that so long as the hunter who first wounded the animal is in "hot pursuit," with the likelihood of overtaking it on account of the nature or severity of its wound, and the animal is killed by a second hunter, the carcass belongs to the one who is in pursuit. But if the wound is not serious enough to interfere with the animal's chance to make a normal escape from his pursuer, the courts have awarded the carcass to the second hunter, even though the first was still following the trail.

After all has been said, it is unfortunate that men who classify themselves as sportsmen cannot settle all such controversies on the basis of the Golden Rule rather than drag the matter into the courts.

It is never ethical for a hunter to lay claim to an animal of a species or sex for which he has no license, even though he has participated as a major party in killing it. This question occasionally arises in parties where varied types of licenses are held by different members of the group. Even though the hunter may kill the animal in question without the aid of another, it must be assumed he killed it for the person holding the valid license for it. This is the only ethical or logical stand that can be taken.

It is often necessary to locate the bullet in the carcass of an animal where a number of persons are shooting at the same one, in order to determine ownership. Sometimes the bullets go entirely through the game and are not available for identification, and sometimes the same caliber of rifle is being used by more than one member of the party, all of which makes identification of the legitimate owner a difficult if not impossible matter. Such questions should be settled peaceably between the parties concerned, or by disinterested persons brought in as arbiters. True sportsmen would divide the carcass at the close of the hunt if another animal was not secured so that both parties laying claim could fill on their licenses.

CHAPTER V

Where and How to Build Camp

IF your main object is big game hunting, don't make your headquarters at some famous resort. On the other hand, if your provisions are made up of a considerable quantity of "Scotch" or other brands of "wet goods," the resort is a much better and safer place to spend the time than is a camp in the wilderness.

Big game animals congregate in greatest numbers as far from the centers of human population as possible. If your primary purpose is hunting, plan the location of your camp accordingly. In the Rocky Mountains and other parts of the West are many cow camps located in high wilderness areas. During the summer months they are used as headquarters for the cow-pokes who ride that particular section of the range.

One of the most satisfactory ways to hunt is to make contact with the owner of such an outfit. He can pack your equipment to one of these comfortable (usually log) cabins equipped with stoves, bunks, and cupboards, and supply you with one of his riders as a guide. It is an ideal arrangement from many standpoints. In the first place, you have more comfortable quarters for inclement weather than a tent could ever afford, and you can leave a lot of duffle at home that you would otherwise have to take along. Another big advantage is that you have access to the most authentic information on the exact location of the game herds. Not the least of the advantages is that you are likely to have available a handyman who can care for horses, pack game in, bring up more provisions as they are needed, and give a lot of very valuable advice.

If you are not lucky enough to make connections for a cow-camp headquarters, these stock ranch men of the mountains may still be secured to pack your camping outfit into

A typical big game hunting camp.

good game country and give a lot of valuable hunting information, in addition to providing horses for packing out your meat when the hunt is over. This will remain quite an important consideration until the time when the helicopter is perfected and in general use so that the hunting party can fly in anywhere and land on the size spot the tent will occupy. The importance of the rancher type of hunting contact has not been fully appreciated by the great majority of American sportsmen.

Of course, the first consideration in locating a hunting camp is to have it close to the game to be hunted. The next consideration is to locate it close to a spring or other suitable water-supply. Generally speaking, most of the running water in big game country is safe to drink. The tent should be pitched on comparatively level ground where trees or rapidly rising ground will provide some protection from prevailing winds. By all means avoid the bottom of a gully, an old stream bed, or any low flat land that may be flooded in the event of a downpour of rain. Also avoid pitching the tent under the overhanging branches of trees. Should it become wet, it will dry out much better in the open. Stake it down securely and dig a shallow trench around it so that surface water, as well as that running off the canvas, will not find its way onto the ground under the tent. This is very important.

A 7 × 9-foot canvas stretched up as a canopy in front of the tent will furnish protection for the cooking operations in case of rain or snow. In extremely cold weather a 7 × 9-foot tent set up inside a 9 × 12-foot tent will provide many times the comfort of a single tent of even the heaviest material.

There are all types of tents available from which to make selections, and the type should be chosen which best meets the requirements for which it is most likely to be used. My own preference in a tent for use any place I have ever camped, is one with a canvas floor sewed into it, regardless of the size or shape of the tent. The floor offers many advantages. It is clean, keeps out insects, is much drier than the surface of the earth, keeps out drafts from below the tent sides, and is a catch-all for small articles of equipment that might be dropped and otherwise lost. In a country where there are mosquitoes and other objectionable insects, have regular mosquito netting attached to the sides of the openings so that it can be readily drawn across.

For one or two persons traveling light, I like a 7 × 9 right-triangle tent with a perpendicular front sloping away toward the back and sides, made of balloon silk or other good-quality, light-weight material. This requires only one pole for setting up, and the pole may be set up outside rather than inside the tent. It may even be set up by tying the top to a tree limb. Some prefer the teepee type tent. The roomiest of all is the regular wall tent, which is recommended if bulk and weight are not major items of consideration.

A typical hunter's camp in the brush country.

Metal stakes occupy less space than wooden ones and are no heavier. They are to be preferred where it is not practicable to cut new stakes at the camp-site. A few nails to drive into the tent poles for hanging lanterns, garments, etc., are handy to have. It is always well to have a couple of extra lengths of ⅜-inch tent rope for emergencies.

Even for the person who expects to do most of his hunting from a base camp where there is a large tent and major accommodations, it is often desirable to make overnight expeditions beyond the range of the main camp. For this purpose the small light-weight silk tent is an added convenience that may be carried in the grub-bag on one's back. For carrying purposes, it is good to have a regular knapsack of the type used by Boy Scouts or even the Army pack-sack.

After the tent has been set up, a great deal remains to be done to assure comfort. The fellow who lays his blankets on the floor of the tent and calls it a bed is either downright lazy or blissfully ignorant or has a glorified idea of being tough. There is no excuse for not having a comfortable bed in almost any country where big game exists. The air mattress is all right if you have one; but my idea of the ideal camp-bed is one made of boughs.

There is a right and a wrong way to make a bough-bed. Most people seem to know only the wrong way. Almost any kind of boughs may be used for a bough-bed, but some type of evergreen is best. If leafless branches are used, much more care must be taken in selecting only the smaller and branchier ones. Those from small bushes, rather than from leafless trees, should be selected. Fir, spruce, or juniper probably make the best beds, although any of the pines will do very well.

Select the bushier branches and break the boughs from the main beam of the larger branch. I prefer to use about 16 inches of the bough tips. These are gathered into the tent in sufficient quantity for the bed. Now cut two poles about 6 inches in diameter and 6½ or 7 feet long, lay them parallel to each other on the floor as far apart as you wish the width of the bed to be, and drive stakes on the outside so they will stay in place. Cut two more shorter poles of the same diameter to place at the head and foot of the bed outline.

Now take your boughs, one at a time, and stand them almost perpendicular, along the pole at the head of the bed. Continue placing the boughs as close together as they will stand until you have filled the enclosure between the four poles. The boughs should lean just enough toward the head of the bed so that when the blankets are thrown on and you climb in, they will all settle forward.

If evergreen boughs are not available and leafless ones are used, it is a good idea to gather dry leaves or grass and pad the top of the bough mattress before spreading the blankets. It will be surprising what a comfortable bed can be made in this way. I prefer a properly prepared bough-bed to an air mattress any time. When camp is broken, the boughs from the bed should be burned to avoid littering the landscape with readily combustible materials.

If folding chairs and table have not been brought into camp, very satisfactory tables and benches may be made by driving stakes into the ground to support small poles 1½ to 2 inches in diameter, each end nailed or bound down, as table-top and bench seats. If conveniences are honestly desired, they are easily provided by a little extra work. Many parties plan to go into the hunting country a couple of days in advance of the opening day of the season in order to have the added enjoyment of hewing a camp out of the rough. It is a wholesome experience for anyone who really enjoys the out-of-doors.

There are other chores, such as enlarging the capacity of springs, or digging a shallow well into boggy ground for the camp's water-supply, clearing the brush away from the camp-site, scouting the lay of the land if the country is new, and many other things that might occur to a hunter. Rifles should be sighted in before leaving for the hunting country. A pole should be fastened between two trees or across the tops of a pair of strong pole tripods for hanging up the game as it is brought in. This should be placed in the shade, if possible. For instructions on camp sanitation, consult Deuteronomy, Chapter 23, 10th to 13th verses.

If a stove is not included in the camp's equipment, a convenient fireplace should be constructed to make the job of cooking easier. Either of two standard types is entirely satisfactory and much superior to the open fire so often used. My favorite cooking fire is one laid in a narrow trench dug in the ground, with iron bars or short lengths of ½- or ¾-inch gas-pipe placed across the top at convenient intervals (the bars require forethought in advance of leaving home). The trench

Cooking breakfast over an open fire.

should be about 4 feet long, 12 or 14 inches wide, and 8 or 10 inches deep. The bars can be spaced at intervals to accommodate the size skillet, pot, pan, or coffeepot to be set on top.

The other type is a stone fireplace built on top of the ground by laying flat stones in two parallel rows close enough together so that the skillets and other cooking utensils will rest on the inside edges of the two sides. This fireplace should be 3 or 4 feet long and at least 8 inches deep. Iron bars may also be laid across the top.

A camp-fire should never at any time be left unattended

until the embers have been extinguished with water, unless the ground is covered with snow.

For the party who employs a guide, it is generally the best policy to depend on him for the location of the camp, the water-supply, and all the other technical arrangements that require knowledge of the country and its peculiarities. This applies particularly if the hunter himself is not an expert. Most guides will do things the hunter's way if the hunter insists, even though they know them to be wrong, because they calculate that, after all, the other fellow is paying the bills and is entitled to make mistakes and do things the hard way if he wants to. Give your guide's advice a lot more than just casual consideration before turning it down.

CHAPTER VI

How to Find One's Way in Woods and Mountains

NEVER a year passes without some hunter losing his life as a result of not knowing how to find his way back to camp or to some other human dwelling. Actually hunters lose their lives primarily because they do not know how to protect themselves from the elements until they are found, or because they overexert themselves in their excitement at being lost, and die of heart failure.

In any event, getting lost is the initial circumstance. In a lot of these cases, the unfortunate hunters have compasses with them. The weakness of a compass is that it has no power to think or reason. If a man doesn't know where he is, a compass is of no value to him.

I have known a lot of men who carry compasses but never consult them unless they don't know where they are. Many of these men will leave camp in the morning not knowing what direction they are traveling from camp. They know they are heading for a certain lake, or ridge, or draw, or canyon, or mesa; but for their lives they couldn't tell you whether it is north, south, east, or west. They have not taken the trouble to ascertain any particular landmarks for locating the camp from a distance. They get into a patch of timber where they cannot see out, or into a fog or snowstorm—and they reach for the compass. Under the circumstances, it is valueless because they do not know what direction they are from camp. The man who expects to depend on a compass must consult it frequently enough to know what direction he is from where he wants to go.

I have carried a small Marble's compass for more than thirty years and cannot recall that I have ever consulted it except to settle an argument with a companion who insisted we were going in the wrong direction. But I have an uncanny sense of direction in the mountains that few have; furthermore, I make mental notes of the general lay of the land—of every natural landmark within the range of vision, of every road and trail shown on the maps of the area. By frequent observation of my surroundings, I know at all times just where I am.

The only time I would have used a compass was when it was in the pocket of another pair of pants. I knew within ⅛ mile of where I was; but without a compass I seemed unable to find my way out. I had come about 15 miles across a mountain, since noon. A mid-December night with heavy clouds and no moon caught me about 5 miles from my destination. In open timber I held my direction without difficulty; but I made the mistake of undertaking a short-cut across a frozen willow bog about ¼ mile wide by ½ mile long and not more than ½ mile from camp. The willows were so thick that it was impossible to go 10 feet in any direction in a straight line. Time after time I would stop and collect my wits for an attempt at orientation; but by the time I had dodged a half dozen willow clumps and stumbled over a fallen aspen log or two, I had again lost all sense of direction. After milling around for half or three-quarters of an hour, I swallowed my pride, fired three shots, got an immediate answer, and was in camp in fifteen minutes. With a few matches and a compass, I would have had no trouble going straight through the willow patch.

If a person is really lost at night and can't get a reply to a distress signal of three shots spaced at two- or three-second intervals, there is just one sensible thing to do: stop where you are and make yourself as comfortable as possible for the night. In the morning you can get to where other people live, if you can't find your bearings for where you want to go. To continue on in the dark is about ten times more likely to take you away from where you want to go than toward it. Furthermore, you dissipate your energy and take chances of stumbling and suffering serious injury. In the meantime, build a fire, if possible, on some prominent point where it may be seen. It may attract attention. If in the morning you are still hopelessly lost, work toward lower ground, follow the first watercourse you come to, and head downstream. It will take you either to a road or to someone's habitation. A local resident can help you find your party.

It should be emphasized that it is much more important to keep from getting lost than to find oneself after he is lost. Here are some tips on not getting lost: when you plan a hunting trip, get a map and orient yourself in terms of the directions from roads, high points of land, water drainages, etc. Then when you get on the ground, make notes of landmarks that can be seen from camp or from some prominence near your camp. Take your compass and study out the directions from camp of your major landmarks. Study the general lay of the land in the vicinity, and especially the drainages as they relate to your headquarters; then don't lose your head. If you aren't sure of your landmarks, depend on a good compass and consult it frequently. One of the errors to avoid is to go beyond your camp on your return from a day's hunt. Many a hunter has got lost after passing his camp at very close quarters.

A rolling plains country is probably the easiest to lose

one's way in while hunting, unless he has made very minute observations as he goes along. For many persons, a close check on a good compass is the safest procedure. Fortunately, there is less big game hunting in such territory than in other types. In the West, antelope are most likely to be found in this type of terrain.

Another difficult type of territory for keeping directions straight is the north woods of Minnesota, Wisconsin, Maine, Michigan and the eastern Canadian provinces, where for long distances there may be few natural landmarks, and where so much of the comparatively flat land is timbered so that one can seldom see out. In such territory one should learn to depend on a compass or some other means of identifying directions.

When the sun is shining, it is not difficult to determine directions when one knows the time of day. When the sky is overcast with clouds so that the sun cannot be seen, it still provides sufficient intensity of light so that it will throw a slight shadow any time between sunrise and sunset. Open a penknife or use the hunting-knife, and stand the point of the blade on the polished surface of a gunstock. Be sure you are sufficiently in the open so that the light will get to it from all directions and that your body does not shut the light from any direction. The blade will cast a shadow that can be readily detected on the polished surface. Don't confuse the reflection of the knife with its shadow.

Persons familiar with the woods can tell which direction is north by examining the bark of trees. The north side of a tree will always have the most moss and other parasitic growth. In the north woods it is very important to know the location of all lakes, streams, and roads in the vicinity to be hunted.

In the wilderness of northern Canada and Alaska the best advice is to secure a reliable guide and stay close enough to him so you don't get lost. You might wear your shoe soles out by trying to follow a watercourse to civilization, and you certainly couldn't hope to find a road to guide you somewhere. The qualities that go to make a guide are not all acquired in a few months, and some of them are probably gifts from birth. Keep these facts in mind when tempted to think of yourself as his equal in wilderness craft.

As a final warning to the man who may get lost from his party on a hunting trip: don't get excited and flustered and start rampaging off in the direction you think might be the right one. Sit down, calm yourself, smoke your pipe if you have one, and look the country over very carefully for some familiar landmark. Give consideration to every aspect of the lay of the land, the drainages, ridges, and the sky-line. If still not sure of yourself, you had better fire a distress signal before going any farther. If you don't get a reply, wait until after sundown and try it again; then build a signal-fire on the highest point you can find. Depend on it that if it can be seen from where your friends are, they will see it. They will be almost as anxious to locate you as you are to locate them.

The farther you go, the less likely you are to be found. In the mountains it is a very easy thing to wander over a divide into an entirely different watershed. Next day, if convinced that you are really lost, better forget your friends and try to get back to civilization. Keep your matches dry and make every one of them count. Never use the last half dozen for lighting the old pipe. They may be the means of saving your life before you get back to your friends.

CHAPTER VII

What to Do in Common Emergencies

THE average hunting camp is likely to be many miles over difficult roads and more difficult trails from the nearest doctor, nurse, or hospital. Yet it is a place where serious emergencies requiring immediate action may originate at any time. Hunting parties are not usually organized around a doctor or a nurse as a nucleus. In fact, doctors frequently flock together on a hunting trip, as a result of which other camps in the vicinity are likely to have no doctors at all. For all I know, this tendency of doctors may be deliberate, for they are on a vacation to get away from sick and injured people for awhile. If we were in their places, we would probably do likewise.

Most hunting is done in country difficult to travel, where there are a thousand things to stumble over; where shrubs and vines and windfall are ready to trip the unsuspecting hunter; where there may be steep banks and steeper cliffs to fall down or over; where stones are ready to turn under one's feet; where jagged tree branches are ready to jab a person's eyes out; where horses are prepared to fall on their riders on slippery mountain slopes, or kick them in the pit of the stomach when they prepare to mount; where knives and axes (in unskilled hands) habitually cut deep gashes in those who wield them; where backs are sprained lifting on heavy carcasses, or trying to break a fall on a slippery rock; where men unaccustomed to the out-of-doors contract "their death of cold" sleeping in drafts and standing around with wet clothing and cold feet; where men get terrific belly-aches from drinking bad liquor and eating improper food (usually the former); where men experience snow-blindness; where gunshot wounds are occasionally inflicted; where an appendix sometimes ruptures; where older men frequently suffer heart attacks; where rattlesnakes, copperheads, and moccasins sometimes find their mark; where feet and hands and noses and ears are all too often frozen; where sunburned and cracked lips are everyday inconveniences, and where skinned shins and broken bones are common occurrences.

The above enumeration embraces a few of the things that might happen to the sportsman on that big game hunting trip. But contemplating it will not discourage many from assuming the risk every time a new open season comes along, even though they swore upon returning from the last trip that it would be the final one for all time.

In view of this persistence of the hunting urge, it is incumbent upon the sportsman to be prepared to deal with the resultant emergencies in the best possible way without a doctor, and to transport the more serious cases to a doctor as soon as possible with the least damage to the patient.

Usually the inconvenience of the patient should not be allowed to disrupt the hunting party by hustling home with the unlucky member. Bind up the strained muscles and sprained ligaments, prescribe cold wet cloths to reduce the fever in the local area, and leave the victim in camp to nurse his own wounds. It will be the best thing that ever happened to some pampered individuals who have always had someone to wait on them at every beck and call.

Daub iodine on the cuts and open bruises. Assign the minor cripples to camp duty to keep their minds occupied. Prescribe complete rest for the eyes of the snow-blinded hunter and confine him to the darkest place possible until relieved. The fellow with a bad cold should be put to bed where he will keep a uniform body temperature considerably above normal. (My own remedy is to dress warmly and walk all day briskly enough to keep constantly perspiring, then come in at night and go to bed with sufficient covers to keep warm. In the morning the cold is invariably gone. This method might not work on less rugged individuals.)

For snake-bite, tie a handkerchief, belt, or cord around the affected limb between the wound and the heart, and keep it tight enough to slow down the circulation radically, releasing it for a short period once every twenty minutes. If the limb becomes numb, take the bandage off until feeling returns. Just as soon as the bandage has been put in place, take the sharpest knife at hand and make two incisions at right angles directly over each fang mark. These incisions should not be less than ¼ inch deep and ½ inch long. Next apply suction with the mouth and draw out the blood and poison as rapidly as possible, spitting out the drainage from the wound. Snake venom is not poisonous if taken internally, so don't worry if some should be swallowed.

After the first two hours, apply suction for only about twenty minutes out of each hour. Don't give a stimulant of any kind for the first twelve hours, and don't give whiskey or brandy or other hard liquor at any time. Coffee is the best stimulant to use after it is safe to use one. It is best to get the patient to a doctor as soon as you can unless there is at hand a complete snake-bite treatment kit. The larger the snake, the larger the amount of poison injected, other things being equal.

If there is a serious cut or wound in an artery, apply a tourniquet between the wound and the heart; and if in a vein, between the wound and the extremity of the limb. Loosen the tourniquet as soon as severe bleeding ceases. Keep the patient inactive and the wound elevated. If not too serious, it will probably heal as quickly in camp as else-where. Keep all open wounds sterilized. A fine healing and sterilization compound has been discovered in the new sulfa drugs which undoubtedly will be used more commonly when available for more general use.

For a gunshot wound through the body cavity, keep the patient lying down and move him only on a stretcher. Get him to a doctor just as soon as possible. A stretcher may be improvised by buttoning two or three shirts or coats over two parallel poles, then spreading the poles apart and binding cross-pieces at each end to keep from squeezing the patient. Lay the patient on carefully and have one or two persons carry each end of the stretcher. One man alone should not attempt to move a person in this condition. Make the injured one as comfortable as possible and go for help. His chances of survival are much better if he remains perfectly quiet. If a main artery or vein is severed internally, there is little that can be done except by a skilled surgeon on the spot at the time of the accident.

Fresh air and plenty of exercise are great remedies for most stomach ailments. Too much liquor is the most common cause of upset stomachs in hunting camps; at least, this has been my observation over considerably more than a quarter of a century. Usually a heaping teaspoonful of baking soda in a glass of water will bring some, if not full, relief.

Soften cracked lips with vaseline or even with lard or tallow. Any type of oil or grease will prevent the air from drying the moisture out of the skin. Blistered feet usually may be prevented by putting on enough socks so that the feet will be well insulated from the hunting shoes. Blisters generally result from friction where the shoe rubs back and forth on the foot.

The fellow with a chronically bad appendix should not be allowed in a hunting camp, for he frequently breaks up the party. If he has a bad attack, better get him out to a surgeon.

Get broken bones in place as best you can, improvise a set of splits and bind them in place. In case of a broken leg or arm, better get the patient to a doctor as quickly as possible. In case of compound fracture, sterilize the open wound and exposed bone. Move the patient as carefully as you can. If a horse is to be had, it is usually better to put the patient in the saddle than to try to move him by hand.

Now for the man who suffers a heart attack from overexertion. The best advice is to keep him quiet just where he is for several hours or move him to camp on a stretcher. In any event, reduce the exertion necessary to get to camp to a minimum, and don't let him leave the camp again during the entire trip, even if it lasts a month or more. You don't want to be handicapped with having to pack out a dead man and spoil a good vacation.

For the chronic grumbler, send him home on foot or insist on his shutting up.

CHAPTER VIII

How to Dress and Pack Game Animals

HAVING been born and reared on a midwestern farm where every bit of meat we ate was butchered at home, I have found it difficult to conceive of anyone not knowing at least the first principles of how to proceed in handling a slaughtered animal. Nevertheless, in connection with my hunting experiences I have contacted dozens of men who had not the slightest idea how to proceed or what to do next when an animal was brought down with a bullet. It is not uncommon to find men who will drag a deer back to camp, or put it on or in an automobile and haul it home, without either bleeding or gutting it. Others will leave the animal just where it fell and go back to camp for help in deciding what to do next.

Every person who goes into hunting country for big game should have a very definite and concrete idea in his mind before leaving home of just how he is going to proceed in taking care of the carcass of the animal he kills, if and when he kills one. No hunter should be dependent on another for the job, even though he has employed a personal guide and cannot visualize being separated from him at a critical period. In actual hunting, it will often be desirable for the guide to make long trips around game while the hunter patiently waits for him to return or for the game to show up; and he may be miles away, or hours away, when the critical time arrives that game must be taken care of without any coaching from anyone.

With the above in mind, it is imperative that the hunter learn in advance how to do the job for himself. One man alone

43

can hang a very large deer easily, as follows: cut a pole seven or eight feet long. Deer and pole are laid parallel on the ground. If the animal is to be hung head up, the upper end of the pole is engaged in a slit in the deer's under jaw. To raise the animal, brace the pole against a rock or stump or the base of a tree, and raise on upper end where attached to head or gambrel stick. As a greater proportion of the animal's weight must be lifted from the ground the angle of the pole approaches nearer the perpendicular, thus decreasing the amount of weight that must be lifted by the hunter. Lean the top of the pole against a tree. There are certain hunters (and most of them have obtained practically all their experience and training in the hunting of birds) who will contend that it is not necessary to bleed a big game animal. Be assured of this: if you want meat of a good flavor and first-class keeping qualities, the animal must be thoroughly bled just as soon after he is down as it is possible to get to him, and preferably before his heart stops beating, since it will assist in pumping all the blood out of the veins. The only time it is not necessary to bleed a big game animal is when it has been shot through the heart or when a major artery has been severed by the bullet; and this isn't likely to happen once in twenty times.

Most experts prefer to bleed an animal by inserting a long-bladed hunting-knife at the front point of the brisket. Thrust it in full length with the blade pointing toward the animal's spine at an angle to insure entering the chest cavity. Then with a semi-circular motion bring the blade crosswise the plane of the chest and sever the major arteries leading from the heart to the neck. The blood should follow the knife out in great pulsating gushes if the heart is still beating. An animal's heart should usually beat for several minutes after it has gone down with a fatal shot.

Never stand on the belly side of an animal or astride either

Whitetail buck hung head down.

its head or its body while sticking it or cutting its throat. (Some prefer to cut the throat from ear to ear, severing the arteries in the neck.) The proper place to stand is behind the animal's shoulder where you can grasp an antler or an ear with one hand while using the knife with the other. In this way the hunter can protect himself and get out of the way without being injured should the animal regain consciousness or struggle convulsively. If possible, drag its head downhill while bleeding in order to facilitate drainage.

As soon as the blood stops flowing, proceed to open up the carcass and remove the entrails, liver, heart, and lungs. Some leave the heart and lungs in but this is a great mistake, for they only hasten spoilage, retard adequate drainage, and may even bring on souring.

In dressing the animal, proceed in the following order: cut around vent or vents below the tail, being careful not to puncture the colon, which should be worked loose from the sides of the pelvic cavity. Next, cut the center line of the belly from pelvis to the rear extremity of the breastbone. In opening up the belly, first make a very small opening with the knife at the very edge of the pelvis. Work two fingers through this hole and press the paunch or intestines out of the way so that the knife will not puncture them; turn these fingers forward along the inside of the belly, insert the knife blade between them, and move knife and fingers forward together. The fingers will act as a shield to prevent the point of the knife blade from puncturing any of the internal organs. Some hunters prefer to use the whole palm of the hand to shield the point.

At this point the hunter has his choice of two methods of dressing the animal out. He may proceed by reaching the left hand into the pelvic cavity as far as possible, and with the right hand pushing the vent end of the colon in until it can be grasped with the left and withdrawn. (In the male animal the penis should have been previously loosened for its entire length and carefully worked away from the rear of the pelvic bone so that it, along with the bladder, will withdraw with the colon.)

Next, roll the contents of the body cavity out on the ground, using the knife to loosen them where they are attached to the backbone for support. When the paunch is reached, pull it out as far as possible and cut the muscles of the diaphragm around its circumference close to the ribs. Press down on the lungs with the left hand, and with the knife in the right hand, reach into the chest cavity and sever the windpipe and gullet where they enter the chest from the neck, and roll out the remainder of the contents.

The other choice in method, and the one to be preferred, is to open up the breastbone (brisket) for its entire length with belt ax or saw (it can be done with a hunting-knife by severing the ends of the ribs separately where they join the brisket). If it is not intended to use the cape for mounting, the cut should be continued on up the lower side of the neck to the throat. The windpipe and gullet should be severed at the throat and worked loose back to where they enter the chest cavity. Now spread the chest, reach in and cut around the circumference of the diaphragm and continue pulling on the windpipe and gullet until the heart and lungs and liver come out; then roll out the paunch and intestines, and finish up by pulling the colon from the pelvic cavity. It will be necessary to loosen the entrails from the back with the knife in the same way as when starting the process from the rear.

If the weather is so cold that there are no flies, the carcass may be propped wide open with sticks to assure a good circulation of air for removing the body heat as rapidly as possible. Pools of blood should be drained out of the depressions in the body cavity or wiped out with a dry cloth; but water should not be used in this process, because the meat is more likely to sour when wet. Hang the carcass off the ground if possible.

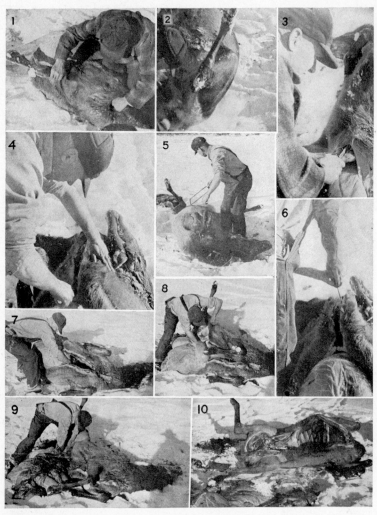

Successive steps in dressing out a big game animal (see bottom of page 49).

In warm weather it is always safest to skin and quarter the carcass on the spot and wrap it in cheesecloth or put it in cheesecloth bags to keep the flies away. Hang in a shady place where there is a good circulation of air. Never leave a carcass without propping it open, regardless of how bad the flies are. You can scrape the fly eggs out later with a knife, but you can't sweeten meat once it has begun to sour. Some hunters carry black pepper and sprinkle the exposed surface of the meat with it, but this is not as safe a method as using cheesecloth.

There are many ways of getting game out of the woods to where it can be loaded onto an automobile or other conveyance. If horses are available, use a packhorse every time; otherwise use what seems to be the best method at hand. Two persons can drag the average deer, hog-dressed (with entrails removed), by tying a cross-stick to the head or horns, with one man grasping each end. The hide is likely to be ruined for nice leather if it is dragged very far. The hardest way is to tie the four legs together in pairs over a pole and swing the pole over the shoulders of two men, but many a deer has been packed into camp like that.

THE SUCCESSIVE STEPS IN DRESSING OUT A BIG GAME ANIMAL

(1) bleeding the animal by severing the main artery between the heart and neck; (2) cutting around the anus in order to loosen the colon into the pelvic cavity; (3) opening up the belly, using the hand as a shield for the point of the knife blade; (4) opening up the skin and flesh along the brisket line; (5) preparing to saw pelvic bones apart; (6) sawing the brisket open; (7) reaching in behind heart and lungs to remove them before removing the paunch; (8) removing paunch and intestines—note the lacelike fat covering the paunch; (9) drawing the colon from the pelvic cavity; (10) the job completed and the animal propped open for proper cooling. In warm weather an animal should be skinned and quartered at once,—and in any kind of weather it is best to hang the carcass off the ground. (*Prepared for publication in* Colorado Conservation Comments.)

The easiest way to man-pack game is to cut it into pieces of convenient weight and pack it out in an ordinary pack-sack on the back. The average man can easily handle two quarters of a normal size deer at a time, or one quarter of a not too large elk, bear, or moose. If the meat must be packed very far, it is sensible to cut it off the bones and leave the skeleton in the woods. An average size doe or small buck deer can be packed whole on a man's back as illustrated; but it isn't safe to do it in daylight where there are a lot of careless hunters.

In preparing an animal to pack in this way, slit the hind legs through the skin between the tendon and the leg bone at the gambrel joints, unjoint the front legs from the inside of the knee joint, and peel the bone away from the skin on the shin for a distance of at least 4 inches. Then shove the right front leg through the right rear gambrel and lock in place with the exposed end of front leg bone. Lean the animal up against a tree or stump (head and shoulders up), sit down on the ground with your back to the animal's brisket, and slip your arms between the looped legs just as you would into the shoulder straps of a pack-sack. Get to your feet and be on your way (in the dark lest some fool should take a pot-shot at you).

If you have a horse with pack-saddle and panniers, the job is easy, however large the animal. Quarter the carcass and load what the horse can conveniently carry. Three hundred pounds is a pretty good load for the average horse. If you don't have panniers, a whole deer or half an elk or moose split lengthwise down the middle of the back can be loaded on either a riding saddle or a pack-saddle by two men without much difficulty, and roped in place.

The westerner would be just about as willing to use a western stock saddle as a pack-saddle for packing game if the carcass has not been quartered. His technique is very simple. He puts the deer, antelope, mountain sheep, or mountain goat across the saddle with the belly of the carcass toward

Most convenient way to "backpack" a deer. It should be done only after fools have gone to camp.

the front and adjusts it so that there is a perfect balance, with the weight equally distributed between the two sides of the horse. With his knife he slashes a slit in the lower half of the belly side of the carcass exactly back of the saddle-horn and within an inch or two of the front edge, raises the place where the slit has been cut, and slips it over the horn.

A pair of veteran packers. The deer are being packed in on regular western stock saddles.

Even without being tied, the carcass will stay in place while being packed home if the going isn't too rough. It is better, however, to tie the legs to the rings in the cinch or tie them together under the horse's belly.

A half elk or moose is handled in exactly the same way— belly side to the front of the saddle and skin side down. No partial carcass packs well unless either quartered or halved lengthwise. When a regular pack-saddle is used, it is not important whether a carcass is loaded belly forward or back forward. My own preference is to load it with the back toward the horse's head and to bind it down with a diamond hitch. With the legs to rear, the carcass is much less in the way in close quarters than when loaded the other way. In any event, the head, if not detached, should be tied up so that it will not swing loose. If detached, it should be tied on top of the load where the antlers or horns will not catch on obstructions and break the points.

As soon as game is in camp, it should be hung on a rack in the shade or on trees nearby where it will not be molested by carnivorous animals. For the purpose of hoisting, a light block and tackle with a 5/16-inch rope for deer and 7/16-inch for elk or moose is a handy piece of equipment. When a carcass is to be left away from camp for any length of time, it is a good idea to tie to it a used handkerchief or a sock that has been worn. The human smell will discourage coyotes, wolves, bears, and other flesh-eating animals for several days. The bear is not as fearful of man's scent as are the members of the wolf family, because he is less likely to suspect a trap.

When it comes time for packing the carcass of game for the trip home, plan to get everything inside a car, truck, or trailer if possible. If there positively isn't room, never drape carcasses over the hood of an automobile or along the front fenders where heat from the motor will start meat spoilage. It is safe to transport meat on the front or rear bumpers or on the top of the car. Cover with canvas to keep out dust and dirt. Where meat is packed inside an automobile, it should be put in only after it has cooled thoroughly, and should be covered with bedding or tent canvas to prevent heat from penetrating it. Keep car windows open for adequate ventilation.

Here is just an additional thought: don't put meat in deep freeze until it has had a chance to hang for at least two weeks where it will not freeze while it has an opportunity to "ripen." All packing-house meat is treated in this way. Don't think meat is spoiled just because it gathers some mold or "grows whiskers." These usually indicate that the meat is beginning to get fit to eat.

CHAPTER IX

How to Skin and Care for Trophies

I BELIEVE I am conservative in estimating that three out of every four big game trophies presented to taxidermists for mounting or preserving are incapable of measuring up to their greatest potentialities because of improper care in handling, owing to either ignorance or carelessness on the part of the owners at the time the animals were killed and skinned. Most of the errors in handling can be grouped under three classifications: improper methods in bleeding the animal; improper methods in skinning out the cape or hood; improper methods of preservation of skins, hoods, and other perishable parts to be used later as trophies.

An animal should never be bled by having the throat cut if the head is to be mounted, because it is almost impossible for the taxidermist to sew up a horizontal gash across the skin of an animal's neck without leaving a distinct line of cleavage in the hair covering the spot. Even where this may be done most skilfully, the lighter colored hairs of the throat are likely to be permanently discolored by blood-stains, which are difficult or impossible to remove from some types of hair when the blood is not washed out with cold water before it has started to dry.

A comparatively small slit made in the skin at the point of the brisket where the knife was introduced in bleeding by the sticking method, can be sewed up so that it will never show in the finished product. Any blood on the hair of the cape to be used in mounting a trophy should be removed by the use of cold water before it has had an opportunity to dry.

There are a few sportsmen who bleed an animal intended as a trophy by plunging a hunting-knife into the animal's heart from its side just behind the front leg; but few men can locate the heart with any degree of precision. Besides, it is very doubtful whether a hole in the heart will drain off as much blood as a severed artery.

An animal to be used as a trophy should be dressed out without splitting the skin up the brisket. Dress out by the first method described in the previous chapter. It is best to remove the cape soon after the carcass has cooled, if inconvenient to do so immediately after it is dressed out. It is much better to include more of the animal's skin in the cape than the minimum that may be used.

I would suggest that the knife be started at the top of the shoulder and the skin opened up to the brisket at a point just ahead of the front leg, with the legs flexed back, and continue on the opposite side until the point of beginning is reached. Now begin at a point exactly over the middle of the spine in the cut above the shoulders; extend the cut along the top line of the neck to about 2 to 4 inches back of the point where the horns or antlers emerge from the skull. Open the skin from this point to the base of each horn.

Next, carefully remove the cape, beginning at the point of intersection of the two cuts above the shoulders and taking care not to cut buttonholes in the skin.

When the base of the ears is reached, cut the cartilage well in toward the skull. Be extremely careful in separating the skin from around the horns or antlers. The novice will do a better job by prying it loose with a screw-driver than by using a knife.

Great care must also be used in cutting the skin away from the eyes to avoid injuring the inner sides of the lids. Gouge deep with the knife into the tear-ducts at the inner corners of the eye-sockets in order to avoid cutting a hole in the skin.

Leave the entire lip on the skin and slit the heavy flesh between the inner and outer lip skin. Leave plenty of cartilage on the skin at the end of the nose. Peel the skin away from the cartilage at the base of the ears and remove all flesh and fat from the entire cape.

Salt the flesh side of the skin very thoroughly, and roll up tightly for 12 to 24 hours, and dry without permitting any wrinkles but without stretching out of proportion. In drying the salted cape it is recommended that the skin of the head be turned flesh side out and stuffed inside with crumpled paper, dried grass, or other porous material.

In former years it was necessary to save the entire skull of antlered and horned game along with the horns; but modern taxidermists require only the top of the skull where the horns are attached. It is best to remove this with a saw, but it can be done with an ax. With the latter, one must be extremely careful not to break the upper portion forming the solid bridge between the horns or antlers.

Blood on antlers of deer, elk, moose, and caribou should be removed with water or snow while it is in a fluid state, since it has a tendency to solidify in the pores of the antler and cause stains that are difficult to remove.

True horn will not be adversely affected. The mountain sheep, mountain goat, musk-ox, and bison are the North American big game animals having true horns. The antelope has a peculiar horn structure not found in any other animal, composed of hair and a secretion somewhat resembling blood. The horn disintegrates very rapidly when exposed to the elements, but is not usually stained by dried blood-spots. Contrary to what many people believe, the prong-horn antelope sheds his horns every year.

The same care as recommended for the capes for mounted heads should be taken in skinning and preserving game skins intended for leather or for rugs. It is best to salt them before stretching out flat and drying, but salting is not absolutely necessary. Salted skins may be folded together, flesh side to flesh side and rolled up for two or three days before being stretched out to dry. Use plenty of salt. Where they are not salted it is imperative to exercise special care to insure that there are no wrinkles and no flesh or fat; otherwise the skin may burn in the wrinkles or under the fat, and the hair is likely to slip.

Skins may be dried by being spread out, flesh side up, on the dry ground, tacked on the wall or hung over a pole. If the last method is used, it must be watched carefully in drying to prevent wrinkles on the legs and near the edges of the skin.

It should be pointed out here that the skins of deer, elk, moose, antelope, and mountain sheep should never be used as rugs to walk on, because the hair is brittle and will very soon be an unsightly object. In fact, walking on any animal skin rug does it no good.

Bear skins intended for mounting into rugs open-mouthed should be accompanied by the entire skull and lower jaw. Don't boil the meat off, for boiling causes the enamel of the teeth to crack. Remove the flesh with knife and scraper and take out the brains through a hole cut in the rear of the skull. Be especially careful to remove all fat from bear skins. Most taxidermists recommend that in opening up a bear skin one should start at the corner of the mouth rather than the middle of the chin.

From there on, the skin is opened up down the underside of the neck and the middle of the belly. Slit the legs on the underside from the pad of the foot to the intersection with the belly edge, and be sure to leave all the toes on the skin.

Skin back to the last joint and salt the inside of the feet well. Otherwise care for the skin as recommended for other big game animals.

The feet and lower section of the legs of many game animals make fine ornaments, gun-racks, lamp-stands, etc. If these are not to be taken to a taxidermist within a few days in warm weather, they should be skinned down to the hoof by slitting along the back side. It is best to clean the bone and leave it intact, for the taxidermist may wish to use it in the finished product.

Do not discard a fine set of antlers because a prong is broken off. Not infrequently an entire antler is shot away. Modern taxidermists can repair them so that the defect will never be detected. If a bear's teeth have been broken, they can be replaced so that the substitute cannot be told from the original.

Some hunters are not aware that the American wapiti, or elk, has a short ivory tusk on each side of the upper jaw. These tusks are present in both cows and bulls, but are larger in the bull. They make very attractive ornaments and should be removed. Usually they have a higher polish and richer coloring in the older animals. At one time members of the Elks Lodge put such a premium on them that it all but led to the extinction of the species.

CHAPTER X

Trailing Wounded Game

THE ability to trail wounded game often means the difference between going home with a fine trophy and a good supply of fresh meat and going home empty handed, disappointed and filled with regret over having wounded a splendid animal and failing to get it.

It is not unusual, while riding through big game country at the close of the hunting season, to find dead animals in considerable numbers lying around where they have died of their wounds, or to see cripples hardly able to make their way around. Most of these would have been tracked down and recovered very soon after being shot had the hunter known some of the fine points of following a trail. Many would have been found if the sportsmen had known even the simplest fundamentals of following a trail. Some of them would have been recovered within five minutes of the time the shot was fired if the hunter had only known how to tell when an animal was hit by a bullet and when not. I have seen men turn to walk away after shooting an animal through the heart, never suspecting that it had been hit, while the animal lay dead not 100 yards beyond.

I once shot the heart out of a deer that ran ¼ mile before it went down with every drop of blood drained from its body. It ran with all the apparent vitality of an uninjured animal; but I knew my front sight was covering its heart when I pressed the trigger and I recognized the dull thud of the bullet's impact. I knew that at the end of the trail there would be a dead buck ready to be dressed out.

On the other hand, more than 50 per cent of the hunters I know would have concluded that they had made a clean miss and would have gone on to look for another victim. I have seen literally dozens of deer run 100 yards or more before going down from a heart shot; and many times they do not even appear to register shock when the bullet hits. Bullets in the brain and in the spinal cord are the only two shots that can be counted on to stop all kinds of big game in their tracks every time, even when shot with our highest power rifles.

My very first experience, more than thirty years ago, with a deer shot through the heart taught me a lesson I have never forgotten: that you must follow game that has been shot at until you are absolutely positive it has not been hit. It was dusk when I saw a buck silhouetted against the sky-line about 60 yards away on a mountain hogback. I could still see the sights, and aimed at the heart. I was too inexperienced to know whether I hit him or not. He bounded off into the brush of the north slope of the ridge. I followed the direction he had gone for 50 or 60 yards and could detect no blood on the bare ground and vegetation.

I stood and listened for fully five minutes to see whether I could detect some sound of his running or struggling, but heard nothing. Concluding that I had missed him, I went home; but all night the thought kept occurring to me that I couldn't have missed him at that short range.

The next morning shortly after daylight I was back at the spot to satisfy my conscience. Not 30 feet from where I had stood and listened the night before lay the head and skin and skeleton of my buck amidst the plentiful tracks of a bear and her half-grown young, where they had neatly skinned him out and filled their bellies on fresh venison chops and steaks at my expense. Never since have I left the trail of an animal I have shot at until absolutely convinced that I didn't hit it, or that the wound was so slight that the animal's faculties were not seriously impaired.

I would warn everyone who hunts big game that, not infrequently, mortally wounded animals may never bleed externally until after they are down, even though they may have traveled considerable distances.

Where there is plenty of fresh snow on the ground that is not badly tracked up, it is not a difficult task to follow game. After they go 200 to 300 yards, they will usually leave a drop of blood here and there if they have not bled externally before. The blood will be most noticeable where they have stopped to look and listen for a few minutes. If you discover that an animal is not seriously wounded, it is better to try to outwit him by guessing where he will go and to intercept him than to follow his trail. He will make it a point to stop where he can see his back trail; and as long as he can continue to go, you are only wasting your time.

If he is badly wounded, you should come upon him in a short distance. When there are a lot of other tracks in the vicinity, it requires very careful analysis of the particular animal's hoof print and gait to be certain that you are on the right trail. The animal may drag one foot slightly, or make a deeper impression in the snow or soft earth with one hoof than with the others, or the spacing of his tracks may be irregular. All these and many more peculiarities may be used in identifying a wounded animal.

When there is no snow and the ground is dry and hard and the wounded animal is bleeding very little externally, if at all, the hunter's powers of woodcraft are taxed to the maximum. He must resort to the tactics of the Indian scout if he would be successful.

A few years ago I trailed a wounded elk with one thighbone shattered for more than ½ mile without ever seeing more than two or three drops of blood in the entire distance. The ground was hard and dry and the vegetation short. Many other elk had been on the same territory. If I had not recognized the thud of the bullet as it struck, I would have been convinced after the first hundred yards of trailing over almost bare rock without a trace of blood, that I had missed him entirely.

When the trail crossed a short strip of ground that had been worked up by moles and pocket gophers, I observed that he placed most of his weight on his right hind foot in favoring the left one. I was careful to observe the slanting dry grass and other vegetation that had not yet fully straightened up since the last animal had passed. After an hour and a half of the most painstaking trailing I jumped my bull out of a depression where he had lain down to rest, and broke his neck as he started to get under way again.

The first shot had been at long range in a heavy cross wind with the animal running at full speed, and he had not noticeably flinched when the bullet struck; but the telltale thud of the bullet unmistakably recorded a hit. It is against the principles of any true sportsman to quit the trail of a wounded animal so long as that trail can be followed.

Wounded game will often circle and backtrack in order to throw the pursuer off the trail; and the hunter must be constantly on the alert to detect this course before spending valuable time retracing steps. A wounded animal will usually break away from his back trail at right angles to his former course, at a point where brush makes it difficult to detect his departure and where other tracks cross the original trail, or on a point of bare rock where tracks are not easily discerned.

In circling, a deer will often cross his first trail with a bound in order to disturb his previous tracks as little as possible. The keen strategy used by some wild animals in throwing pursuers off their trails is truly amazing. Seldom will a wounded animal stop to rest where he cannot observe his back trail for a perfectly safe distance, to plan his escape.

It is only the badly wounded animal that you may hope to get within sight of while following his tracks. Where two or more hunters are in the party it is always a good idea for all but one to try to outguess the wounded animal by intercepting his probable course. This last one follows the trail to insure that he will not hide in some secluded spot and allow the hunters to pass, sometimes at very close quarters, without seeing him.

Of course, dogs are ideal for trailing wounded game, but most states do not permit them to be used in any capacity in big game country. In trailing wounded game it is best to pursue an animal just as rapidly as possible that is shot through the lungs or bleeding profusely. The reason is that exercise taxes the lungs to their maximum and also stimulates bleeding. But if the animal is shot through the paunch, intestines, or heavy muscular parts of the body such as hind quarters, or even the muscles of the neck, it is best to sit down and wait an hour or two before engaging in extended pursuit. The reason is that inactivity causes lameness and stiffness and distress in the injured tissues and discourages continued flight.

CHAPTER XI

Effect of Moon and Weather
on Game Animals

ABOUT 90 per cent of the sportsmen with whom I am acquainted hold the opinion that the effect of the moon and weather on success in hunting is mostly, if not wholly, a matter of pure superstition.

I have put in many a hard week of hunting in order to discover the truth in regard to the matter. As a result, I can say with positive conviction that if it is "mere hunting" one is interested in, he may totally disregard all natural phenomena. In fact, if one wants an excuse to be in the field a long time without too great a chance of filling out his license right away, he can select the proper time to accomplish this end; but most sportsmen are interested in either early success or an opportunity to look over a maximum number of animals in the hope of selecting an exceptionally fine trophy. These persons should study the calendar before planning to hunt.

Most big game animals do the greater part of their feeding while the moon is overhead. This holds true whether the time be day or night. Exceptions to this rule are the daylight feeders—sheep, goats, and antelope—which are likely to be most active early and late in the day.

For most big game hunting a good rule is to let the restless, the ambitious, and the ignorant tramp the woods and mountains alone, from the time of the month that the moon rises about sundown until it begins rising at around 1:30 or 2:00

o'clock in the morning. Of course, these restless fellows will kill some game, but in the aggregate they will do a lot of hunting to get it, and most of the successful ones will be "lucky" only because they ganged up on the animals and drove them out of their beds past other hunters stationed at favorable locations to intercept them. Once in a while a still-hunter will spot an animal lying in its bed, which thinks it will be overlooked; but most game will sneak away to safety long before the hunter arrives in sight.

In areas where the law allows only a few days of open season, the hunter, of course, must make the best of the situation regardless of the environment Nature has created. Where the law provides a sufficiently long season, the wise hunter, if he plans a two-weeks trip, will set up his camp when the moon rises at about 2.00 A.M. and be sure that the red gods will not interpose their displeasure. For the first few days he should hunt from daylight until 10:00 or 11:00 o'clock, and again for an hour or two about sundown. Unless the rut is on, only the females and young are likely to be feeding a second time during the daylight hours.

When the moon rises about daylight the best hunting will be the first four hours after daylight and the last three or four hours before dark, although game is likely to remain more or less active during the entire day. When the moon doesn't rise until about 2:00 o'clock in the afternoon, the hunter who is not looking for a lot of hard work might as well stay in camp for a little nap after his midday lunch.

While the game animals are bedded down they have nothing to do but cat-nap at intervals, chew their cud, look, listen, and analyze every faintest scent that the changing air currents bring in; and they do an exceptionally thorough job of detecting the first signs of danger. The hunter has to be mighty nature-wise to outsmart them.

When animals are feeding, the tables are turned in favor

of the hunter and against the hunted. Every step the animals take interferes with their hearing of sounds farther away.
They are seeking the sight and smell of choice foods with eyes
and noses. In other words, the animals' senses are devoted
primarily to seeking food instead of detecting the presence
of enemies.

They feed with their heads down or behind bushes or
weeds or clumps of grass, and their ears are filled with the
sounds of swishing branches and crunching browse being
reduced to sizes that can be swallowed. The wise hunter
will take advantage of all these natural factors that work to
his good in seeking big game animals. The careful hunter
can approach within a short distance of feeding game if he is
careful to move only when heads are down.

There are general weather conditions that also have a
bearing on the sensitivity of animals to the dangers surrounding them. High winds that whistle and moan through the
tree-tops without much opportunity for the changing zephyrs
of a quiet day, distract attention from the hunter's movements
and scents. Fog and drizzling rain dull the senses of smell
and soften the leaves and twigs that might crunch beneath
the feet. Deer, in particular, seem to dislike lying down in
the first snow of the season if they are moving around at the
time it falls, and may wander restlessly long after their customary time to bed down and seek quiet.

Naturally, snow is a great aid to the hunter. I have observed that after a heavy snowfall game animals seem to
be just as reluctant to start moving about, if lying down at
the time snow is falling, as they are to lie down in the first
fresh snow of the season. It is not infrequent to observe
where they have remained in their beds for forty-eight hours
after a severe storm, without getting up to feed. Under such
conditions they are very hard for the hunter to find, since
there are no tracks to indicate their proximity.

A long stretch of extremely dry weather will make every leaf and every dry twig and every blade of grass and every weed, and even the soil under one's feet, cry out in alarm at each step the hunter takes. In such weather the animal's senses respond much more readily to every vibration of whatever kind, carried to them through the air.

The one who must hunt under such conditions should be especially careful of the type of clothing he wears. Soft moccasins for the feet and, externally, woollens for all parts of the body should be the order of the day. Even so, it is better to seek out a likely place and remain quiet while the game does the moving, with but a few members of the party assigned to keep them on the move.

During dry, noisy weather game animals will usually move into dense cover where they can more easily elude hunters whom they will locate at long distances. Here they avoid exposing themselves without the necessity of crossing open spaces in hiding from their pursuers.

After exceedingly dark, cloudy nights, even when the moon is favorable for night feeding, they will almost certainly do some feeding just at daylight and again at dusk. The hunter should be prepared to take advantage of every favorable break provided by Dame Nature. To do this he must familiarize himself with the feeding, sleeping, and living habits of his quarry.

CHAPTER XII

A Guide's Place in the Hunting Party

THERE are sportsmen who do not fully understand the relationship that should exist between themselves and the man whom they employ as guide. It is not surprising that this is true in view of the fact that so many guides have been imposed upon by a few conceited snobs who looked upon them as menials or valets.

The average guide is just as good as the man who employs him. He is probably just as much a professional specialist as the lawyer, surgeon, or bank president who retains him. The fact that his education has followed entirely different lines than that of the average person who hunts, is the very factor that makes his knowledge valuable.

The first principle that should be accepted in every hunting camp is that all shall share equally in the camp chores, unless someone has been specifically employed as cook and camp tender. The guide should never be considered as cook, horse wrangler, packer, and general flunky. If there is no one employed to manage the horses or if they belong to the guide, his part of the camp chores should, of course, be the taking care of the horses. Where this is the case, don't expect him to cook, wash dishes, carry water, chop the wood, and do all the other camp drudgery. For the man who desires to do nothing in camp but lounge around and smoke and take life easy, I would advise taking the required number of servants along on the trip.

The sportsman has a right to expect that his guide will be a woodsman or a mountaineer or both; that he will know the terrain to be hunted (unless you have insisted upon his going into unfamiliar territory); that he will know how to make a comfortable camp out of a minimum of civilized gadgets; that he will know the habits of the game to be hunted; that he will know how to dress out and care for game meat; that he will understand how to care for game trophies; that he will know how to pack and handle horses; that he will be cheerful and congenial unless he is being imposed upon.

Most big game guides do not depend upon guiding as the entire source of their livelihood. Many of them are the owners or foremen of cattle or sheep ranches, or backwoods farms, or they may be professional trappers or engaged in some other frontier occupation.

The duties of the guide will vary with the type of party he is with, and with the wishes of the men who employ him. Some men prefer to employ a guide who will devote his entire attention to their own personal hunting problems. In such cases the guide's duty is clear: to be his employer's "Man Friday" and accompany him everywhere, constantly giving the advice and assistance desired. Such a guide is likely to have a minimum of strenuous work to do but he is almost certain to be called upon to make some very important decisions that involve a lot of responsibility.

He must be able to estimate distances where a wrong guess of 50 yards would put a bullet over or under game instead of into a vital spot on the quarry. He will often be called upon to estimate the length and spread of an animal's antlers or horns, by a hunter who will be very much disappointed (as well as angry) if he "wastes his license" on a trophy that won't qualify for a place in the "upper twenty" listed among the world's record heads. He may be required to make decisions on just where a fleeing animal may next emerge into view. It is well for the sportsman to keep the fact well in mind that no man living can always give the right answer to all these questions.

After all has been said, if the hunter hopes to merit the title "sportsman," he will realize that most of the answers should be his and not his guide's responsibility. Too many so-called sportsmen are only killers who depend upon a guide or someone else for all the skills required. These occasionally include even the shooting of the game.

This introduces the next question to be discussed, one that has been argued pro and con on a basis of ethics ever since hunting licenses came into use. Not infrequently law and accepted ethics are in opposition to each other on the question. Where this is the case, the law is difficult to enforce. Most states interpret a hunting license as authorizing only the person whose name is written thereon actually to kill the animal that may be lawfully possessed under the license. Sportsmen in all parts of the country regard this interpretation as a violation of the fundamental ethics of the chase since time immemorial.

In many districts where game (deer in particular) are taken through the process of driving, where large parties participate, and where frequently only the best shots are assigned to the shooting stations, it is expected that they will continue to shoot as long as legal game appears in sight and the entire party's quota is not filled.

In the West where stalking or still-hunting is the favored method of hunting, the common practice is for no one during the early days of the hunt to shoot more game than his own individual license permits. But if some members of the party fail to fill on their licenses up to a short time before the hunt is to be concluded, it is quite generally conceded that, with the consent or at the request of the holders of the unfilled licenses, it is perfectly ethical for other hunters of the same party to take a hand in the shooting.

The foregoing is neither more nor less than to provide the general background for the commonly accepted rule governing the relationship between the guide and his employer. When requested to do so, most guides can see no ethical reason why they should not help out in filling on licenses, regardless of laws to the contrary. It is probably unfortunate that lawmakers have not always been practical-minded men with wisdom enough to avoid the passage of statutes that they may reasonably expect will be violated in a wholesale manner.

Having interjected these explanations, we return to the question of a guide's proper procedure under other circumstances than when serving a single person. It should be obvious that the greater the number of individuals in his party, the less the attention that may be given to each. If the party is large, the guide should not be expected to do more than advise the individuals on where game is most likely to be found, and on other matters where assistance is needed, and help in packing in the game where no one else is in charge of the horses.

The guide of a large party not using packhorses should not be expected to assist in bringing in game the hard way (by man power). Usually the men of a party who have filled on their licenses assist others as required. This is just a matter of general hunting camp courtesy.

In planning for a hunting trip where a guide is employed, it is customary to depend upon him to make all necessary preliminary arrangements of a local nature. This may include the transportation of equipment to the site of the camp, setting up of tents, etc. If the party desires to eliminate as many camp chores as possible, the guide may arrange to have camp wood cut in advance.

The guide is entitled to his regular rate of pay for the time spent in making preliminary arrangements, as well as reimbursement for all expenses incurred, including rental on packhorses and other transportation required in carrying out the wishes of his party. He is often entrusted with securing the necessary licenses for the members of his party. In such event the money should be sent him with the request, for many of these hardy men work on very close monthly or weekly margins. At best, even the well-to-do rancher is not likely to have a large cash reserve at a given time.

Above all, the guide is entitled to be treated as an equal in every way with other members of the hunting party, for the great out-of-doors recognizes no line of caste or station or creed. Every man must stand or fall on his own merits as a human being, and frequently the man with the largest checking account must be rated at the bottom of the list.

In the hunting camp only the knowledge of nature counts, and the guide is almost certain to be the most highly educated of the group. His standing within the camp should be judged on this basis alone, regardless of his table manners, his dress, or his grammar.

CHAPTER XIII

The Whitetail Deer

THE whitetail deer is one of the shrewdest of North American animals; in fact, I would classify him as the shrewdest hoofed animal on the continent. Even in the face of advancing civilization he has been able to hold his own in thickly populated areas with a minimum of protection. Of all animals of North America commonly classed as big game, only the bear may be considered more clever in dodging the hunter. Other hoofed animals may be rated more difficult to hunt, but that is only because the terrain they inhabit is more difficult for man to cover and because they range over more extensive areas.

The whitetail deer has the faculty of dodging a dozen hunters in 40 acres of cover without ever leaving the tract, whereas the mule deer might run several miles and the elk leave the entire county to evade his pursuers. I once trailed a wounded whitetail for four hours in hot pursuit without his getting farther than ½ mile from the starting-point.

I know of no better sport than matching wits with a wary old whitetail buck (still-hunting), where the game resolves itself into an individual contest of skill. I have consistently refused to participate in organized drives on these noble animals because, to me, that lacks all the fundamentals of sportsmanship. However, it is recognized as a standard way of taking them, and most of them are killed through this type of hunting.

Before taking up specific details of hunting procedure it is well to review the habits of the proposed quarry. The whitetail deer is a lover of dense, heavy cover, of brushy river-bottoms, of swampy lands well covered with clumps of cedar, willows, and other vegetation tall enough to conceal

Whitetail buck.

him. When not hunted, he likes the forest fringes bordering cultivated lands.

In the West, even where their range extends into the mountainous country of northwestern Montana, northern Idaho, and British Columbia, the whitetails avoid the more open hillsides except when feeding at night. Unlike most of our other species of big game animals, they seldom migrate more than 3 or 4 miles between their summer range and the location where they may yard up for the winter. Apparently they would rather starve to death near their customary haunts than

seek better food away from home. In northwestern Montana
I have seen hundreds of mule deer migrate directly through
a whitetail range without stopping, except to browse a little
along the way. But the whitetails never followed them out
in the fall, or back to timber-line in the spring.

The common whitetail deer varies more in size in the different parts of his range than do any other members of the
deer family. In the extreme southern part of his range he
will not average much more than half the weight of those
at the northern extremity, where he may occasionally hog-
dress as much as 300 pounds or more.

This deer, wherever found, is distinguished by a broad tail
with long brown hairs fringed with white above and white
hairs on the underside. When running he invariably erects the
tail and waves it slightly from side to side, giving the appearance of a white flag. If struck by a rifle bullet while running,
he brings the tail down with a convulsive movement.

Whitetail deer are somewhat lighter in body color than
the western blacktails; however, they vary somewhat between their southern and northern ranges, being usually
lighter in the south and darker in the north. Their ears are
much smaller than those of the mule deer of the West. The
antlers of the whitetail buck are formed of a gracefully
curved main shaft from which rise rather evenly spaced
spikes pointing slightly forward of the perpendicular. The
points vary in number on mature bucks from three to six or
seven on each main beam. Occasionally they will have additional short lateral points.

The range of the whitetail is from the Atlantic seaboard
to the Pacific, and from Old Mexico nearly to Hudson Bay.
At present there are very few whitetails west of the Rocky
Mountains, except in the lower part of their range and in the
Columbia River drainage. Of the Rocky Mountain states,
Colorado is probably the only one where the whitetail has

been entirely exterminated, although Wyoming has but a very few of them left.

In their eagerness to classify everything, scientists have confused the subspecies of the noble whitetail deer in the various sections of his immense range until they can't agree even among themselves on the matter of where one subspecies leaves off and another begins.

The food of the whitetail varies greatly over his extensive range. Basically he, like other members of the deer family, is a browser, living on the twigs and shoots and branches and leaves of favorite plants. He is fond of garden truck, mushrooms, moss, berries and other fruits, acorns and other nuts, grains, and a variety of weeds and plants. In some places his winter food is largely made up of white cedar browse, while in other places it is constituted almost entirely of the leafless twigs of various types of trees and brush.

The man who would successfully hunt the whitetail deer should constantly bear in mind that the fellow he is looking for is probably more interested in dodging him and silently slipping back into the cover he has just hunted, than in getting away from him by going ahead into new territory. I have passed whitetails within 15 feet when they were lying down in good cover and thought I would not detect them.

It takes a well-organized drive to push deer out of thick cover without some working back during the process. Most game will quit an area when intensively hunted, but the whitetail usually prefers to stand his ground and match his wits against his pursuers.

I recall one occasion when seven or eight guests had hunted for about ten days from the old Montana ranch and still lacked three deer of filling on their licenses. They were worn out and discouraged. I saddled a horse I could shoot from and in two hours hung up three bucks, none of which was farther than ¾ mile from the ranch house, on ground that had been tramped over every day for ten days. The difference was a matter of experience in hunting these elusive strategists plus the advantage of the additional elevation of a horse's back.

In most of the eastern half of the United States the white-

The author's first buck. Taken in Flathead County, Montana, and registered with Records of North American Big Game.

tail deer is hunted by men in packs. This type of hunting requires that the terrain be studied very carefully in advance. Every natural runway must be observed and evaluated with the idea of selecting a place where a man stationed with a rifle, or with a shotgun loaded with buckshot, will be most likely to get a shot at a deer trying to escape ahead of those who have surrounded the cover to be driven, and are advancing noisily through it.

A prominence high enough to allow the hunter to look down into the cover below is always good. A narrow opening such as an old logging road, trail, or open face of a narrow ridge is excellent. Care should be taken that hunters are not given stations where they will be required to shoot toward one another.

Sometimes a swamp with many small openings affords a good place to station the man who is to do the shooting. An old burn usually affords many favorable locations. The crotch of a dead tree may be the ideal place for the shooter to conceal himself so that he has a broad view of the territory where deer are likely to cross. In this kind of hunting it is customary for a hunter who has made a kill to become a permanent member of the driving crew, thus giving everyone a better chance to kill his own game.

In the heavily hunted areas in the eastern part of the country it is not uncommon to require sportsmen to hunt from regularly established and supervised camps where a limited number of men are allowed at a time. On the other hand, I have hunted days at a time in the Rockies without encountering another hunter.

The real sport of hunting the whitetail is to be realized only where every sportsman goes his own way and depends on his own wits and judgment and strategy to outsmart his quarry. In attempting this, the nimrod will take into consideration the direction of the wind and will always avoid going down-wind where the game might get his scent. He will choose a type of terrain where the cover is sufficiently broken that his chances of getting a shot at fleeing game are at least fair, and where he may hope to see far enough ahead that the quarry will not have seen him first. Sometimes the hunted expose themselves while trying to make sure whether friend or foe is approaching.

Instead of going through noisy underbrush it is usually

advisable to select trails or roads or the edges of swamps or damp ground where clothes do not rub against vegetation, and where the shoes make a minimum of noise. In the West where the whitetail is accustomed to heavy livestock, such as cattle and horses, moving about through his cover, one may sometimes have better success barging through the brush with no attempt at being quiet. The one who hunts this way, however, must be blessed with extremely good sight so as to spot the game before it identifies him as a human being, or be an exceptionally quick and accurate shot on running game.

A great many local residents of western range areas hunt from horseback and pay little attention to the amount of noise or to the direction of air currents. A perspiring horse apparently has such a strong odor that he practically blots out the scent of his rider.

The general principles discussed in this chapter hold true whether the hunter is in the great north woods, the southern canebrakes, the hills of the eastern states, the Panhandle of Texas, or the mountains of the West. No one can ignore the habits of the game he is hunting, and hope for success.

The whitetail, like all other game animals, may be successfully hunted merely by selecting a favorable locality where other hunters are moving about, and settling down for a perfectly peaceful but extremely observant day. Sooner or later such a hunter will surely be rewarded for his patience; but the hunters who are willing to pay the price of long hours of inactivity, fearful of making a move that might attract the attention of a pair of alert eyes somewhere back in the brush, are few and far between. The deer is a far better waiter than the average hunter. One of the most successful hunters of my acquaintance is a cripple whose friends take him into game country where he merely sits quietly all day.

The question of where the hunter should place his bullet in game is often debated around camp-fires. No single answer can be given because some men can place a bullet where they wish, and others can't. This is true even of a lot of expert target shots. A deer doesn't carry a target consisting of a little black dot surrounded by concentric circles. The most conspicuous thing some people see about a whitetail is the white flag that takes the place of his tail when he starts to run. When waving over his back, it makes a conspicuous target, but its center is about 6 inches too high to be effective for bagging game.

The center of the shoulder is the safest place for the nervous novice to aim, because it has the largest vital area around it and a bullet off center in any direction will still strike in a vital spot. A bullet through the shoulder will ruin considerable meat. The heart lies low and just back of the shoulder. Most excited persons shoot high, which makes a heart shot a good choice because there is from 12 to 16 inches of vital area directly above it. The bullet may strike the lungs or liver and stop the animal in a short distance.

No one should ever aim at a point on a game animal back of the diaphragm. For the hunter who can place his shots where he wants them, the best place to aim is at the intersection of the skull and spine. Some prefer to break the neck farther down. A neck or head shot will drop an animal in his tracks and destroy a minimum amount of meat. A shot aimed at the neck that does not sever the spinal cord is not always fatal, however.

The choice of a rifle for whitetail deer is a matter which should receive serious consideration by everyone who hunts them. In my opinion, based on many years of hunting, nothing delivering a smaller shock at 100 yards from the muzzle than the .22 Savage High Power should ever be used. This cartridge is loaded with a 70-grain bullet and is also the lightest weight bullet that should ever be used on game the size of deer, despite its rated energy.

Don't use any of the high-velocity .22-caliber varmint rifles on deer. The rated foot pounds energy of the .22 Savage High Power cartridge is 955 pounds at 100 yards. Theoretically, it is considerably less than that of two of the newer .22-caliber super-speed varmint cartridges; but their lightweight bullets of less than 50 grains and explosive character will not always assure penetration to the vitals of a deer even when it is shot in the shoulder.

Several of the older cartridges such as the .38–55 would be adequate on deer, in spite of their lower theoretical energy, if it were not for their low velocity and resulting high trajectory, which are responsible for many misses on standing game and many gut shots on running game.

For a detailed evaluation of rifles and cartridges for various types of game one would do well to consult the author's book *The American Rifle for Hunting and Target Use* (The Macmillan Co., 1944, $1.95).

For short range shooting in brushy country the .30–30 Winchester and .30 Remington, which are ballistically identical, are hard to beat in spite of the fact that the load is more than fifty years old. The .30–40 is more powerful than necessary but is an excellent brush cartridge. Both the .25–35 Winchester and the 25 Remington are adequate for whitetails, and the .250–3000 Savage is about as near the last word in deer rifles as will ever be built.

The 87-grain hollow-point bullet in the .250–3000 Savage is not surpassed by any cartridge in use today for killing qualities on such game as deer; but it is almost useless in thick brush since it will go to pieces on impact with twigs. But the 100-grain Winchester Silvertip bullet in this cartridge will do a very satisfactory job in brushy country, because it holds together exceptionally well.

The .30–06, .270 Winchester and other cartridges of their class are much more powerful than required for whitetail deer, and their heavy recoil is objectionable to many persons. For the person who owns but one rifle and expects to use it also for elk and larger game, the .30–06, .270 Winchester and .300 Savage are ideal choices.

A rack of northern whitetails.

CHAPTER XIV

The Mule Deer

THE mule deer belongs to the blacktail family and is the largest member of that species. In some parts of his range the mule deer is commonly known as the blacktail. He is distinguished from the whitetail in being usually a little darker in color and in having a light-colored patch of hair on the rump, a narrow light-colored tail with no hair on the underside and tipped with a black tuft. He is a little larger than even the northern whitetail and runs with the tail down and with a peculiar high bouncing or bounding gait when startled (landing on and taking off on all four feet at the same time). His ears are extremely large and his antlers have prongs which almost always branch in pairs, so that each main prong forms a large Y as contrasted with the single pointed branch of the whitetail. The average mule deer buck will dress out from 25 to 50 pounds heavier than the average northern whitetail.

Roughly, the range of the mule deer extends from the foot-hills of the Rockies into the Cascades, and from New Mexico, Arizona, and southern California into the northern Rockies of British Columbia. In northern United States and southern Canada it extends east of the Rockies and into western North and South Dakota and Nebraska; and in Colorado the range in the northern and southern parts of the state reaches almost to the Kansas line.

The habits of the mule deer are very different from those

of the whitetail. Even where their ranges overlap, the two species are very seldom found in the same environment. Mule deer do not usually stay in thick brush unless they are feeding on the acorns of scrub oak or are being hunted with great intensity. They prefer open timber or even open hillsides, with here and there a clump of aspen or other cover

A pair of Colorado mule deer bucks. The buck in the lead is an exceptionally fine specimen with as fine a rack of antlers as I have ever seen.

into which they can retire if occasion demands. They may even choose to range in sagebrush many miles from trees.

They seldom frequent dense forests, although they may often be found on the open tops of ridges bordered by heavy timber. During the summer and early fall the old bucks are usually in greatest numbers in rather inaccessible places in high country, sometimes even above or just at timber-line. A favorite haunt is under rimrock, where such a formation is close to adequate cover to which they can retire if danger threatens.

In bedding down they almost always seek a location where they can observe the country for a considerable distance, and where there is a ready exit in at least two different directions. Does and fawns usually stay nearer water than do the bucks, and feed out from heavier cover.

Like the whitetail, the mule deer eats practically no grass but lives almost entirely on browse. Fronds and coarse weeds of various types are eaten in considerable quantities in the summer months, but browse of a variety of kinds constitutes the major portion of the year-round diet. Both the large and small sage are favorites; scrub oak, mountain mahogany, sarvis and rabbit-brush are staples wherever found, and Oregon grape seems to be rated as a special delicacy. Many types of brushy shrubs and plants are eaten to some extent, and juniper is browsed heavily in some areas. When food is scarce these deer will browse on almost any of the evergreens. The flesh of the mule deer is neither so fine textured nor so palatable as that of the whitetail.

Owing to his habits, the mule deer is hunted in quite a different manner from the whitetail. In addition to a rifle of flat trajectory, the hunter should provide himself with a pair of 6- or 8-power binoculars. Because of their preference for more open country it is often possible to locate mule deer feeding on semi-open hillsides a mile or more away. I have many times located them even when they were bedded down on exposed prominences far beyond rifle range. The last one I killed was stalked after he had been observed bedding down at a distance of about three quarters of a mile. Certainly it is not at all unusual to observe the mule deer much farther away than one can detect antlers. In consequence, the hunter without glasses is very much handicapped.

One of the finest bucks I ever saw was in the company of

four other deer feeding on a brushy hillside late one evening, at a distance of about 400 yards. I located him in the glasses and then raised my rifle. The four were constantly changing positions, and by the time I started to aim I was uncertain which was the one with the record set of antlers. Eventually, after many a check and double check, they fed out of sight without my firing a shot. That was one occasion when I wished for a moment that I had a telescope sight on the rifle —something that is nothing but a nuisance ninety-nine times out of every hundred. I once had a 330 Weaver mounted on one of my rifles but found it so inconvenient and so unreliable in many ways that I gave it away. A peep receiver sight with almost any good front sight will get the hunter more game in the long run.

A great deal of brush upon which the mule deer feeds is lower than the animal's back, thus making a buck very conspicuous as he goes along bobbing his antlers up and down while reaching here and there for choice bits of browse. For this reason a favorite method of hunting is to find a convenient lookout position from which to study exposed areas of acceptable browse during the feeding hours—usually early in the mornings and late in the evenings. This requires patience in excess of that which many of us possess. Plans should be laid in advance for stalking such game after it has been located, if out of reasonable range for the type of rifle being used.

Many parties hunting the mule deer prefer to employ a method representing a modified form of the drive so frequently used in hunting the whitetail. The members of the party will line up from 100 to 200 yards apart and move forward in unison through typical broken country dotted with clumps of cover that might conceal deer. As the animals are forced to flee across open spaces, someone of the group is almost certain to get some shooting; and in many instances a half dozen riflemen will be shooting at the same animal at the same time, all from different angles.

Where persistent hunting has driven the mule deer to cover, he can sometimes be hunted successfully by placing members of a party on runways while others of the group comb the cover, as in hunting whitetails. A great many westerners hunt the mule deer almost entirely from horseback, by riding parallel through areas where the deer are known to be located. Usually no shooting is done from the horse's back unless at very short range.

A favorite way to hunt the large old bucks in the rimrocks is for the hunter to follow the tops of the rims as quietly as possible, always taking the direction of the wind into consideration. At convenient location he should peer over the rim, exposing himself as little as possible while studying the terrain below for one of the shrewd old fellows bedded down or feeding, as the case might be. It is a good idea in this type of hunting to station one or two men at crossings where the bucks might be expected to escape if disturbed. The object, however, is not to disturb them if it is possible to avoid doing so until the shot is fired.

The mule deer can be hunted very successfully by the still-hunting method, since they can usually be seen at much greater distances than their whitetailed cousins, owing to the difference in their customary habitat. It is probable that the hearing of the mule deer is slightly better than that of the whitetail and that his sense of smell is equally good. Neither species has long-range vision so far as detecting stationary objects is concerned. On the other hand, anything that moves is almost certain to be observed and studied until its identity is determined. In making his analysis, a mule deer may almost completely circle the object to get its scent. Although he may not be as shrewd in some respects as the whitetail, the mule deer is a worthy match for any sportsman's skill.

Most mule deer migrate considerable distances from their high-altitude summer ranges to their winter ranges in the foothills. Some of these migration routes are only a few miles, while others are from 60 to 100 miles. The famous White River herd of western Colorado was given considerable publicity in the writings of Theodore Roosevelt. Its migration route for the most remote individuals on the summer range may actually exceed 100 miles. About 20,000 deer make this migration every spring and fall. About 1,000 deer crossed the upper part of our old Montana ranch on a 30-mile trek to and from their summer range.

It is only natural that hunters should take advantage of these seasonal movements when they occur during the open hunting season, as they do in many places. About all a hunter has to do is sit down behind a clump of bushes along the trail and eliminate all the hard work. In a sense it hardly deserves the title of hunting, and may be but very remotely related to sportsmanship; nevertheless, thousands of hunters get their deer every fall in this way.

In selecting a rifle for hunting the mule deer, a low trajectory up to ranges of 300 yards or more is highly desirable. Four exceptionally fine cartridges with trajectories of 6 inches or less at 300 yards are the .250–3000 Savage with 87-grain bullet, .257 Roberts with 87-grain bullet, .270 Winchester with 110- or 130-grain bullet (the 110-grain preferred), and the .30–06 with 150-grain bullet.

Another excellent cartridge is the .300 Savage with 150-grain bullet. In the lower-velocity, higher-trajectory class of suitable cartridges are the .25–35 and .25 Remington, .30–30 and .30 Remington, .30–40, .33 Winchester, .35 Remington, .348 Winchester, 405 Winchester and 8 mm Mauser. With the exception of the .30–40 and 8 mm Mauser, none in the low-velocity group should be considered as suitable for long-range shooting.

CHAPTER XV

The Pacific Coast Blacktail Deer

INCLUDED in this chapter are the blacktails of California, Oregon, Washington, and British Columbia, and the closely related deer of the southeastern Alaska coast sometimes differentiated as the Sitka deer.

Aside from the fact that the deer in its northern range is somewhat smaller than it is farther south, there is no essential distinction between the animals or their habits. Both the Pacific Coast Blacktails and the Sitka deer are smaller than the mule deer, and their ears are smaller in proportion to their body size. Their body colorings average slightly darker than the mule deer and their antlers are much smaller, although they have the same characteristic branching common to all members of the blacktail family, which includes the mule deer.

All the Coast blacktails are primarily dense-forest dwellers. Like the whitetail deer they are to be found in heavy cover, whence they emerge only to feed along the shore-line or in small clearings close to cover. They are less often found in open areas than is the whitetail.

Although size may be thought of as the principal distinguishing characteristic between the mule deer and other members of the blacktail family, it is also true that the coastal deer have much more hair on the tail than does the typical mule deer. They also have hair on the underside of the tail.

Seton says that the blacktail deer is "a small specialized

form of mule-deer that has taken to life in the heavy timber of the rain belt." The ranges of the two overlap in the Cascade Mountains of Washington and in southern California, where there is evidence of interbreeding. In captivity the mule deer and blacktail readily interbreed; but the whitetail is not known to cross with the mule deer or the blacktail, either in captivity or where their ranges overlap.

Pacific coast blacktail deer.

In general, the range of the blacktail deer consists of a strip of Pacific coastal land about 200 miles wide and 2,000 miles long. They are seldom seen farther inland than the summit of the Cascade Mountains. They are very numerous on the islands off the coast of southern Alaska and are found as far north as Chichagof, Baranof, and Admiralty Islands. Their numbers are estimated to have reached 3,000,000 head in primitive times, but in the 1880's hide-hunters reduced their numbers to a low point from which they gradually increased under protective legislation.

Like other species of deer, blacktails are largely browsers, but during the rainy season they paw up and feed on roots. They also feed on various species of fungi that are numerous in the coastal area. Like the whitetail they are fond of certain types of moss and other parasitic plants. On the coastal areas they consume considerable quantities of seaweeds.

The flesh of the blacktail deer, like that of the mule deer, is much less palatable than that of the whitetail. It is neither so fine grained nor so well flavored. When in its prime and properly aged and cooked by one who knows how to prepare it, it is acceptable to most people; but there are many who do not care for it in any form.

Methods of hunting blacktails are, in general, very different from those effective for hunting their close cousin, the mule deer. A great deal of what has been said about hunting the whitetail is applicable to the western blacktails, although the latter can scarcely be considered as clever at evasion tactics. The denseness of the vegetation over much of his range, however, is often a compensating factor in favor of the blacktail in his contest with the hunter. For this reason I consider the whitetail the easier of the two to hunt, especially by organized drives.

The most successful method of hunting the blacktail is by cooperation among a considerable number of hunters organized to drive the deer out of the brush and past others stationed at strategic points. On account of the type of country in which they are usually found, they are harder to stalk than the whitetail throughout the greater part of their range. Anyone who has made the acquaintance of the devil's club of our western coastal regions can readily understand some of the inconveniences involved in hunting blacktails. In cut-over land where the new growth is not too high, it is sometimes possible to hunt them successfully by following high ground where the hunter has a view of adjacent hillsides or across ravines, or where he may look down into lower terrain.

Along the tide-flats the easiest way to hunt the blacktail is to conceal oneself along the marshy flats where he comes to feed early in the morning or late in the evening. Apparently there is sufficient salt in the tidewater vegetation to make it a more attractive part of the diet than the browse farther back from the beaches. I have often observed blacktails in considerable numbers along the Alaska beaches when the sun hung low on the horizon at either end of the long northern day.

Except where these deer are hunted along the open beaches, a rifle of high velocity and low trajectory is not especially desirable, for the bullets are more likely to be deflected by intervening vegetation. In dense cover, even the shotgun loaded with single slug or large buckshot is sometimes as effective as the rifle.

Among rifle cartridges well adapted to these deer are the .25–35, .30–30, .30–40, .300 Savage, .30–06 with heavy bullets, .33 Winchester, .348 Winchester with 250-grain bullet, .401 Winchester Automatic, .35 Remington; and for close-range shooting in brush the old .45–70 is hard to beat. For hunting on the open beaches the .250–3000 Savage, .257 Roberts, .270 Winchester with light bullet, and the .30–06 with 150-grain bullet are ideal weapons.

CHAPTER XVI

The Wapiti or American Elk

THE wapiti, more commonly known as elk, is the largest of the world's round-horned members of the deer family. By a considerable segment of the world's sportsmen the head of a big bull elk is considered the most magnificent of all hunting trophies. As a matter of fact, a large elk rack is too high and too broad to look well on the walls of a modern living room or den. Even the head of a massive moose occupies small space in comparison with that of the wapiti.

When the white man first came to America the range of this splendid animal extended across the continent and well up into southern Canada. Since the elk had little to fear from most predators, he occupied the plains country as well as the forests and the mountains. Like many other species of game he early yielded the open country before the westward migration of the man with the rifle, and sought protection in the forests and in the mountain fastnesses. Today he is seldom to be seen far from timber cover where he can flee for protection from the hunter.

For a time it looked as if the elk might be headed for extermination along with the bison, except as a curiosity in zoos and parks. On account of his immense size and the fine flavor of his flesh (which is much more palatable than that of any other member of the deer family), he was much sought after by the market hunters of the early period of western development. Even in the most remote districts he was pursued and slaughtered by the thousands when snows became so deep that he could no longer travel.

Protective game laws arrived in time to prevent the elk from sharing the fate of the buffalo; however, his recovery was much slower than that of the deer. One of the principal

Bull elk on the move.

contributing causes was that he had a pair of useless tusks in his upper jaw that had become the official emblem of a na-tion-wide organization of men who were in the beginning neither sportsmen nor conservationists. With an exorbitant price for "elk's teeth," hundreds of thousands of animals were slaughtered for their tusks alone by unscrupulous poachers in defiance of the law, and the carcasses left to rot where they fell. It was only after the lodge repudiated and condemned the practice and ceased to make a fetish of the tusks that the herds were able to start on the spectacular come-back that has placed them on the open hunting list of many western states. Even in some of the eastern and southern states there is a possibility of the wapiti again becoming a recognized big game animal. Right now a few are being hunted in limited areas.

At the present writing, 1945, Wyoming leads the nation in the number of elk, with Colorado, Montana, Idaho, Washington, Oregon, and southwestern Canada harvesting large numbers annually. A few additional states have large enough herds to sell a few licenses each year, with prospects of extensive hunting in the near future. The wapiti is probably the hardiest and most versatile of our big game animals and if given a fair chance will hold its own against heavy odds.

Unlike the smaller members of the deer family, the elk is not an exclusive browser but gets along well on a diet of grass and can even survive on hay for extended periods. If given his choice of feeds, he will select browse and grasses in about equal amounts. During a hard winter elk have been known to survive for long periods on nothing but the bark of aspen trees.

Today most of North America's elk have been forced into the higher and more rugged areas. Winter surveys of herds have frequently revealed from 50 to 75 per cent of the total number wintering on windswept ridges above timber-line in the Rocky Mountains. There are few localities where they can be hunted successfully on foot from a place where an automobile can be driven. Saddle-horses and pack outfits are almost a requisite for success in elk hunting, where a pack of 15 to 30 miles is not unusual.

There has been a lot of loose talk to the effect that hunting elk is "about as much sport as going into a neighbor's pasture and shooting his Jersey cow." This thought had its origin at the time hunting was first opened up after a period of com-

Early morning picture of elk from the air.

plete protection ranging from twenty to forty years. It is true that the initial hunting took the animals completely by surprise, since they had learned to pay little attention to the presence of men. Today it is a different story wherever they have been hunted. Anyone who doubts this should reflect upon the fact that the hunter success-ratio is lower on elk than on deer in most states where both are hunted with no restriction on the number of licenses sold.

Under hunting conditions the habits of elk and deer are very different. A hunting camp set up in deer country at the beginning of the season will still be in deer country when the season closes. But a hunting camp set up in the midst of a herd of 300 head of elk on the opening day of the season may be from 20 to 50 miles from the nearest elk by the evening of the second day. I have known a herd of about 75 head of elk that traveled almost 45 miles in nearly a straight line before they stopped after the first shooting started; and when they stopped, it was in heavy timber containing so much windfall that it was almost impossible for a horse and rider to get through.

Last fall I rode for three days without seeing an animal in an area literally covered with fresh tracks of elk. They were in heavy timber on steep mountain-sides, and no amount of riding or coaxing would induce the animals to venture into the open.

The elk's senses of smell and hearing are very nearly, if not altogether, as keen as those of the deer; and my personal observation leads me to believe that his sight is even better, although inferior to that of either the mountain sheep or the mountain goat. To say the least, his faculties are a fair match for those of the best of hunters, and the sportsman who gets an elk trophy under present-day conditions will usually more than earn it.

Methods of hunting elk must be adapted to the type of

country in which the animals happen to be located. Regardless of the character of the country, the average distance at
which elk are shot is much greater than for deer in the same
type of cover. One reason is that the elk are larger and can
be seen farther away. Likewise, the game can identify the
hunter at a greater distance. Another reason is that the elk

*Horses are a necessity in successful elk hunting over most of
their present range. On the "Hermosa" in Southwestern Colorado.*

is by nature less likely than the deer to hang around for a
second look. He is also less likely to take chances on hiding
out with the hope of being by-passed and not detected.

In much of its western range the elk is to be found in fairly
rough country where small open parks are interspersed with
clumps of evergreen trees and aspen or scrub oak thickets. A
favorite procedure for the hunter in such country is to locate
an area of fresh elk sign from horseback, then tie the horses
and proceed on foot, taking advantage of the lay of the land,

with the individuals of the party spreading out to make the
most of the possibilities at hand. If there are natural lines of
travel ahead, one or more hunters should be dispatched ahead
to cover these points. Elk are often located on opposite hillsides or high ridges far beyond effective rifle range, and must
be carefully and intelligently stalked for many miles if the
animals are on the move. A knowledge of the terrain over a
large area is extremely valuable in hunting them. Much of
this type of stalking is done on horseback, with the hunter
dismounting only when he is in position to shoot.

For hunting in heavy timber on steep hillsides, horses are
practically useless. Best results are to be obtained by or-
ganizing a considerable party to keep the animals on the move
while other hunters are stationed at likely places where the
game must cross openings or ridges. An intimate knowledge
of the lay of the land is absolutely essential in this type of
hunting. Where herds have been broken up and badly scattered, they may be taken by the same type of still-hunting
methods as used on deer. Often, if a person will spend most
of his time just sitting down in an inconspicuous place, others
hunting in the same area will keep the game on the move; and
eventually the patient waiter profits most.

During the light of the moon it is extremely difficult to
hunt elk where there are very large areas of dense black
timber; but in the dark of the moon they can be found early
in the morning and late in the evening feeding in aspen groves
or at the edges of open parks bordering the dense forest.
Snow for tracking makes elk hunting much easier in any
environment, since they usually travel in herds of considerable
size and their general whereabouts can readily be determined
by the freshness of the tracks.

The elk hunter should go into the field prepared to do a
real butchering job. The deer hunter knows that if required
to do so, he can hoist his animal off the ground single handed

and move it as required in the process of dressing and load-
ing. With elk it is an entirely different proposition. The
cows will sometimes go above 600 pounds, live weight, and
bulls occasionally go beyond 1,000 pounds. One cow killed
in Colorado last year weighed 636 pounds just as she fell, and

Six hundred pounds of elk ten miles from camp.

dressed out 466 pounds. This is a heavy load for two pack-
horses. A large bull may sometimes dress out as much as 700
pounds. Even two men, without block and tackle, cannot
hang a large elk off the ground.

If not properly cooled at once, the flesh of an animal as
large as an elk will almost certainly sour, except in very cold
weather. Every hunter should be prepared to halve the carcass lengthwise, or quarter it on the spot as soon as it is
dressed. For this purpose most experienced hunters carry a

small meat saw or belt ax, the former being preferable. If flies are still about, the halves or quarters should be wrapped in cheesecloth or slipped into cheesecloth bags and hung up off the ground. Regular packing-house tubing is even better than cheesecloth, if it can be secured.

The skin of the elk does not make such fine-quality leather as that of the deer; but it makes up well into jackets, riding chaps, indoor moccasins, and many other useful articles. The top grain is much more easily snagged than buckskin but the leather is tough and durable. It is not a desirable glove leather. The skin of the legs with the hoofs attached, and tanned with the hair on, make attractive novelty rifle scabbards. I have made a number of them for myself and my friends. The hoofs of the large bulls can also be made into ash trays and other gadgets.

In selecting a rifle for hunting elk, one should choose a cartridge of the low-trajectory class, for distances in elk country are usually very deceiving. A great many western guides use the .250–3000 Savage almost exclusively. It is a remarkable little rifle and in the hands of the experienced hunter is entirely adequate for elk. It is especially well adapted for use by women and others who dislike the heavy recoil of larger calibers. I have killed more elk with it than with any other caliber, and never lost an animal that I hit with it.

For the average hunter, I would recommend a cartridge with greater energy, even at the expense of the extremely flat trajectory. In a lever-action rifle, the .300 Savage unquestionably tops the list, since it combines flat trajectory with adequate shocking power. Select the 150-grain bullet in one of the controlled expanding types, if available. Even the .30–30 has killed and will continue to kill a lot of elk.

In a bolt-action rifle the .30–06 with 150-grain controlled expanding bullet cannot be excelled. The .270 Winchester with

130-grain bullet is a close second and provides an extremely flat trajectory. Other good rifles are the .30–40, the 7.9 mm Mauser, the .348 Winchester with 250-grain bullet and the .300 and .375 H & H Magnum loads, both of which are unnecessarily powerful for elk.

In an automatic, select the 401 Winchester, the Remington chambered for the .300 Savage cartridge, or a military arm using the .30–06 cartridge. The .35 Remington automatic cartridge will kill elk, but its trajectory is bad and its energy is rapidly dissipated. It was designed for comparatively short-range work. Never use the .30-caliber army carbine for elk or any other kind of big game animals.

CHAPTER XVII

The Moose

MOOSE are the largest of the deer tribe. They vary in size and color in various parts of their range. Those of Alaska are the largest, and those of the southern limits of their range are the smallest.

They inhabit the Rockies into Wyoming and occasionally one is killed in northern Colorado. Their present range extends across the continent from ocean to ocean above the northern boundary of the United States; and in addition to the Rocky Mountain area, as indicated above, they are to be found along the marshy areas of our northern border from Maine to Washington, with intermittent gaps. The northern limit of their range is well toward the barren wastes of the far north.

Bull moose have been killed that would weigh between 1,600 and 1,800 pounds and dress 1,000 pounds or more. In height they will stand from 6 feet to nearly 8 feet at the withers. Seton records one killed in 1918 that measured 8 feet 7 inches "from heel to hump." Probably very few of them will actually stand more than 7 feet tall, and in all probability not many large bulls will weigh more than 1,200 pounds, live weight.

The moose is a denizen of the lake-shores, marshes, and muskegs, seeking cover in the fringes and clumps of timber close to his favorite foods, which consist of browse and the succulent vegetation of lake-shores and swampy areas. Much

Alaska bull moose.

of the food in summer is secured from under water, and he may frequently be seen feeding with his head entirely submerged. He is exceptionally fond of lily pads. One of the staple foods in winter is willow and other brushy browse. In some places in Alaska and the far north moose have been observed on high windswept ridges above timber-line. This, however, is not their customary type of environment; but when the swamps and lakes are frozen they will seek brushy areas for food, where travel is least impeded.

The American moose is a close relative of the European elk and undoubtedly would have been called the American elk had the early French and English explorers been familiar with the European species. The antlers are broadly palmated and extremely heavy. Unlike the wapiti with antlers rising high above the head, the moose has antlers that extend almost horizontally and sometimes reach a spread of more than 6 feet in extreme cases.

Another peculiarity of the moose is the "bell" under the throat, which is usually from 4 inches to 2 feet long. The longest on record was 38 inches. Its purpose is not known, although some surmise that it may be intended to intercept and divert the water from the chest when the animal raises its head from feeding under water.

Moose are still very numerous over much of their original range in spite of heavy hunting. They increase more rapidly than the wapiti, because they usually have twin calves as compared with less than 10 per cent of twins among the wapiti. Like the elk, they have few natural enemies other than man, although wolves and lion prey on them occasionally.

Moose do not ordinarily migrate with the seasons, but they may gradually drift over considerable distances as favorite foods become scarce owing to overuse or other causes. Unlike the wapiti, they are not usually found bunched except during the winter months when yarded in the deep snow.

From what has already been said, it should be evident that moose hunting is quite different from hunting most other North American game animals. Swampy terrain bordered by dense timber and often grown thick with willows and other rank vegetation, in itself offers obstacles difficult to surmount. The moose is a good wader and a good swimmer, and hunters have never developed a type of amphibious locomotion satisfactory for following him. Man must take his choice between hunting where he can get with a canoe and where he can get on foot. Much of the actual swampy habitat he will find impracticable to penetrate by any method during the open hunting season. It is, of course, possible but not always practicable for a party to combine or coordinate the land and water approaches to the problem of getting a moose.

The method of hunting moose at night from canoes with strong lights is now illegal in practically every part of the moose range. A great deal of hunting is still done from canoes. A skilful paddler can propel a canoe with almost no noise to attract the attention of the average moose, deer, or bear in the vicinity. I have approached them to very close quarters around the bends of northern rivers without their having any suspicion of my presence.

Along streams or lake-shores where there are lily pads or other choice food, they may be hunted very successfully from canoes if the season opens before the freezing of the water. Should an animal of this size be killed in the water, it is a difficult task to get him ashore where he can be dressed and butchered in a satisfactory manner. Hunters often experience a great deal of difficulty in getting the flesh of the moose out to where it can be conveniently transported back to civilization. Unlike the territory inhabited by the elk where horses are usually available for packing, moose country may be hundreds of miles from such a convenience. Even where horses may be had, the nature of the land surface often is such as to make travel by horse impracticable.

The best time for hunting moose is early morning or late evening, although during the dark of the moon they may be found feeding at almost any time of day. In areas where they are more or less intensively hunted, they are prone to do

Wyoming bull moose in velvet.

most of their daylight feeding in secluded spots where they cannot be approached without sufficient noise to warn them in time to stage a get-away.

The moose may be successfully still-hunted where the territory is made up of broken ridges and intermittent open parks. But in much of his range these conditions do not prevail to any very great extent. Where they do exist, the hunter will be wise to follow the high ground as carefully and quietly as possible, keeping on the alert for every sound or movement that might indicate the location of his quarry.

As the moose moves around in feeding, he often makes considerable noise in shallow water or dense brush. If close, one may frequently detect the dripping of the water from his muzzle or from his "bell" as he raises his head from feeding under water.

I am convinced from personal observation that the eyesight of the moose is less keen than that of either the deer or the elk. At distances of even a few feet he is apparently incapable of recognizing a human being unless he sees the person move or gets the man's scent.

The moose may be successfully hunted by being driven out of thickets and clumps of timber through open territory that he must cross in making his escape. By stationing hunters at such strategic places the chances of getting the animal are sometimes very good. In fact, many moose are killed annually through this strategy.

During the rutting season the male moose is sometimes a dangerous animal, and the hunter attempting to drive him from dense thickets must assume a greater risk than in other types of hunting. A man is at a great disadvantage in making his way through low brush when compared with the long-legged, massive brute he is hunting; and there are plenty of records of hunters being killed by wounded or enraged bulls. A bull may choose to stand his ground and fight in preference to running from cover. He may also be passed up at fairly close quarters without being observed.

Probably the best method of hunting moose during the mating season is by calling them up to the hunter through an imitation of the mating call of either the cow or the bull. If the call of the bull is employed, the oncoming animal is likely to approach in a fighting mood. In any event an approaching bull is likely to make plenty of noise, so that his whereabouts are pretty well known most of the time. Since moose-calling is an art requiring long practice, there is no reason here to go into details of the process or of the general characteristics of the calls. A good many hunters have been killed by attempting to stalk a calling moose. In some instances two hunters have been calling and answering each other, each believing the other to be the moose. The man doing the stalking is usually the one to be killed. Never attempt to stalk a moose you have been calling if you want to live.

Hunting moose by calling them up is coming more and more to be considered unsportsman-like. Furthermore, it is being legislated against as an illegal practice in some jurisdictions. Even where it is still legal, it obviously has the disadvantage of being most effective during the mating season when the animals most merit protection. Many sportsmen refuse to kill moose even when called up by their guides, contending that it is no more a matter of sportsmanship than shooting a domestic bull in someone's barnyard.

The flesh of the moose is one of the choice game meats. I would have difficulty distinguishing a prime young moose steak from a good beefsteak. The skin of the moose is extremely serviceable and is probably the choice of all leathers for moccasins. It is much tougher than that of the wapiti or American elk and of a much less spongy texture.

It is possible that more moose have been killed in the past forty-five years with the .30–30 Winchester cartridge than with all others combined, for it is the "crossroads store" ammunition of the greater part of the moose's range. In comparison with more modern loads, the .30–30 is too light for game of this size; however, little complaint has been made of its killing qualities, since most moose are killed at comparatively short range. Rifles such as the .250–3000 Savage and .257 Roberts are deadly killers on moose in the hands of an expert, but can hardly be recommended for the novice. The principles applying to the selection of a rifle for elk hunting are almost reversed in choosing an ideal weapon for moose hunting. The elk or wapiti is likely to be jumped from cover at long ranges and killed while running at top speed, thus requiring a bullet at high velocity with flat trajectory. This implies the desirability of sacrificing bullet weight in favor of increased speed in the selection of an elk rifle.

The moose, because of his greater bulk, requires greater bullet penetration; and the fact that he is most likely to be encountered at comparatively close range makes a heavy bullet, even at a lower velocity, a better choice for the moose hunter. The fact that the moose may also be encountered in dense brush makes the selection of a heavy slug of lead doubly desirable because of its tendency to maintain its course better after coming in contact with such obstacles as limbs of trees and brush.

In lever-action rifles, the .300 Savage using the 180-grain bullet and the .348 Winchester with the 250-grain bullet are the top numbers on today's market. The old Model 95 Winchester in either .30–40 or .35 Winchester calibers is an old standby that has been hard to beat for the last fifty years. Many hope it will again be put on the market. In the .35 caliber its cartridge is very nearly the same ballistically as the .348 with the same weight bullet (250 grains).

Among the automatic rifles suitable for use on moose is the Remington chambered for the .300 Savage cartridge, or the .35 Remington cartridge, which is decidedly inferior to the .300. The Winchester's Automatic in .401 caliber is also an excellent moose rifle. The .30–06 with 220-grain bullet, if it will function in our military automatic, the Garand, is a very good choice.

In the bolt-action class of rifles there is a wide range to choose from. In all of them, when hunting moose, the hunter should provide himself with ammunition loaded with the heaviest weight of bullet with which the particular shell is regularly loaded. Among the cartridges especially suitable for moose and for which bolt-action rifles are regularly chambered, are the following: .270 Winchester, 7 mm Mauser, .30–40, .300 Savage, .30–06, .300 Magnum, 8 mm Mauser, .375 Magnum. The last named is actually more powerful than necessary and is primarily adapted for killing grizzly bears, big Alaska brown bears, and African big game.

CHAPTER XVIII

The Caribou

THE caribou, like the wapiti and the moose, retained one of its Indian names because its first discoverers among the white men were not acquainted with its European relatives. The caribou is nothing more nor less than the reindeer in his New World range. He is the most docile and tractable of the deer family and in Europe has been domesticated for generations. There is less difference between the Old World reindeer and the average American caribou than there is between the American caribou of the Rocky Mountains and those of the Arctic barrens.

The American caribou range in size from the far northern members of the species, whose large males will seldom weigh more than the largest whitetail bucks of northern United States (300 to 350 pounds), to the large mountain caribou, whose males will sometimes weigh as much as the average male wapiti (600 to 700 pounds). Other than size and a gradation in coloring, there is not a great deal of difference between any of the types.

Although the hair-splitting scientists have attempted to separate the caribou into twelve or fifteen subspecies, there are in reality only three: the woodland caribou, the mountain caribou, and the barren ground caribou. Even among these the gradation is so gradual that no one can say positively where one subspecies leaves off and another begins. In this respect the situation is similar to that of the whitetail deer.

Roughly, the range of the caribou is from the northern border of the United States to the islands off the north coast of North America, and from the Atlantic to the Pacific. At present there are very few of these animals below the 49th parallel of north latitude.

It is impossible to give an exact definition of the areas

Caribou bull.

occupied by the three major divisions of the family; but most of the so-called woodland caribou live in the part of Canada lying south of Hudson Bay and east of the Rocky Mountains, while the large mountain caribou inhabit the Rocky Mountains to their northern limit, and the barren ground caribou range north of the heavily timbered areas of the continent. In size the woodland caribou occupies a place about midway between the other two.

As to the number of caribou in North America at the present time, probably no one is qualified to speak with much authority; but their total numbers are presumably greater than all the other members of the big game species combined. It has been estimated that there are more than 30,000,000 head of barren ground caribou alone, living in a vast interior expanse of territory beyond the reach of all conventional methods of travel. Tens of thousands of hunters may swarm to it by airplane within the next decade; but in the past it has been practically a closed chapter in the sportsman's book. Even as this is written, well-authenticated reports are coming back from the far north of whole herds of caribou being wiped out wantonly by our northern Air Force personnel in target practice from both fighting planes and bombers.

The caribou differs from other American members of the deer family in a number of particulars. Unlike other species, most of the females have antlers, but somewhat smaller ones than those of the males. The antlers are usually palmated on the ends, and a palmated "shovel" branches forward over the top of the nose. An extremely large pair of mountain caribou antlers may exceed 5 feet in length, with a spread of 4 feet. The males universally shed the antlers earlier than the females.

In comparison to its size, the legs of the caribou are longer than those of any other member of the deer family excepting the moose. The hoofs are very rounded and larger, in terms of the animal's weight, than those of any other hoofed animal. It is estimated that it has 1 square inch of supporting hoof surface for every 2 pounds of its weight, as compared with only 1 square inch for every 8 pounds of weight in the moose.

In going over snow or boggy ground caribou can use the whole lower leg from the toes to the hock to walk on. In other words, they carry a pair of snowshoes with them all the time. In traveling they seldom vary much from a straight line, but prefer to swim lakes rather than to go around them. The normal swimming speed is said to be about 3 miles per hour and they have been pushed to 6 miles per hour. The broad feet make exceptionally fine paddles, and the buoyancy of their coat causes them to ride higher in the water than any other animal, thus reducing the friction in swimming, thus assuring them first place among hoofed swimmers.

In August and September the coat of the caribou is extremely soft and almost silky. But as the hairs grow longer, they enlarge at the base until they form a solid mass of hollow tubes so close together that they are forced to stand out straight from the body. There is also a fine short undercoat of oily wool that is impervious to water.

The large hollow hairs, each providing a perfect air space, are the most complete insulating material to be found on any animal in the world; and in terms of warmth are the lightest weight of any blanket provided Nature's four-footed children. They also form a perfect life preserver when the animal is in the water. In his winter coat, it is impossible for the caribou to sink, even when dead.

Naturally, the skin of the caribou provides the inhabitants of the far north with practically everything needed for clothing, as well as with materials for winter dwellings. For many Indian and Eskimo tribes the caribou provides practically 100 per cent of the necessities of life—food, clothing, and shelter. In my opinion, the flesh of the caribou is inferior to that of the whitetail deer, elk, and moose. In flavor and texture I would compare it with that of the mule deer.

Unlike any other members of the deer family the caribou is on the move almost constantly. The great migrations of the American bison were probably no more extensive than those of the caribou. Like the bison, caribou travel in great herds, migrating many hundreds of miles as the season progresses—north in spring and summer, and south in fall and winter.

The woodland caribou probably averages shorter distances in the migration cycle than do either the large mountain or the small barren ground types. A peculiar phase of their migrations is that there are always small scattered bands to be found the year round over most of their range, from the farthest north to the points farthest south.

An aspect of their migrations which has the most direct bearing upon the hunter's problems, is that their migration routes seem to rotate over a long period of years. The hunter may find them following a route many many miles from the place where they trekked through by the thousands only the previous year. This is especially true of the barren ground caribou.

The fact that the winter food consists very largely of lichens, which are extremely slow in growth, probably accounts for the drifting habit of the species. It is said that caribou may suddenly show up on a range where they have scarcely been seen for twenty or thirty years. The Indian tribes of the far north are necessarily nomadic, since they must depend upon keeping in touch with the caribou for their livelihood.

Probably the caribou will never be hunted extensively by the sportsman except for the head as a trophy, or for the sheer novelty of the trip into the great north, in which case hunting will serve merely as an alibi. In the past such a trip has meant long weeks in a canoe on almost unknown rivers, where a man may travel for months and never meet another human being.

In the near future, guides and outfitters with airplanes may take the place of the sturdy frontier guide at the paddle of a canoe. If this is the case, a northern hunt may become less strenuous by far than the average hunting trip into any of our western states. The game herds could be located from an airplane, and the hunter might well be set down beside the trail or deposited in an air-inflated rubber boat amidst thousands of swimming caribou. There he could sit and study the animals for the finest heads as they swam by at about 3 miles per hour, and finally take his choice and have its floating carcass picked up from the water by an amphibious plane.

In hunting the woods caribou when they are scattered in small bands, much of what has been said about the hunting of moose is applicable, except that the caribou is much more inquisitive and can easily be called up or stalked from behind, since he usually travels straight into the wind. The mountain species is the hardest to hunt because these animals are usually found above timber-line in rugged mountain pockets. Often they may be associated on the same range as mountain sheep and even mountain goats.

Once located, they are not difficult to approach, because over most of their range they have never met up with a man and a gun. Of course, in the districts where they are hunted most consistently, such as the Cassair district of northern British Columbia, they become more "spooky" and must be approached with considerable care.

When I was living in Wrangell, Alaska, the port of departure for practically all hunting expeditions into the Cassair, I saw the Stikine River boats loaded with caribou antlers piled high on the decks as well as on the tops of the boats' cabins. The Alaskan Highway may some day provide more ready access to some of the best mountain caribou range; but the Stikine River is likely to continue to be a popular route into the country, since it offers one of the most picturesque river-boat trips in the world.

To hunt the barren ground caribou once one has arrived at the scene, is little more exciting than shooting domestic sheep out of a flock being driven along the highway. A reasonable degree of care is advisable in approaching the herd; but after once getting concealed behind a rock or other natural feature of the landscape, the hunter may study

Preparing to unload trophies from Stikine River boat at Wrangel, Alaska. The heads and horns came from the famous Cassair big game district of British Columbia and were loaded at Telegraph Creek, British Columbia, head of navigation on the Stikine River.

them by the hour while they are in migration without exciting much attention so long as he remains quiet. When the bands are not engaged in migration small groups may be enticed to close range by waving a white handkerchief or even by bleating. They are probably even more curious than the pronghorn antelope in the days of the white man's first entrance upon the western scene.

As a matter of fact, the sportsman who takes a barren ground caribou trophy will usually do it as deliberately and cold-bloodedly as a western sheepherder selects the lamb for his next week's mutton chops, because it is not in the least in the nature of a sporting proposition. Just one word of advice: don't hunt in the North until the insects are gone, unless you have a hankering for being eaten alive. I haven't!

What rifle should one use on a caribou hunting trip? No one is likely to hunt exclusively for caribou, so my advice is to select a rifle and a cartridge adapted to the largest of the species of game you expect to take and use it on the caribou as a matter of convenience. Usually the .30–06 or the .300 Savage cartridges are excellent choices in whatever type of arm you prefer. For the bolt action, the .30–06; for the automatic or lever action, the .300 Savage.

If the largest additional game in which you are interested happens to be sheep and goats, any one of the following is entirely adequate: .250–3000 Savage, .257 Roberts, .270 Winchester, or either of the two calibers listed above. They all have comparatively flat trajectories. If you are looking for moose in dense thickets, or for grizzlies or Alaska brownies, it is best to plan on carrying a rifle that delivers a long, heavy bullet that packs a lot of wallop. I should recommend nothing lighter than the 8 mm Mauser with 236-grain bullet. The best of the big bear rifles are the .30–06 with 220-grain bullet, the .300 H & H Magnum and the .375 H & H Magnum. The hunter who is sure of himself and is a good shot can afford to pack a lighter rifle, but others should depend on fire-power.

CHAPTER XIX

The Pronghorn Antelope

THE pronghorn antelope is almost as exclusively confined to continental United States as the caribou is to the territory above the 49th parallel of north latitude. There is only a very slight overlapping of the pronghorn's range into either Canada or Old Mexico. Strange as it may seem to the average person, the outside boundaries of its range are very little changed from what they were when the white men came, although the outside fringes are now pretty thinly spotted.

Pronghorns are and always have been exclusively animals of the plains and pasture-lands. They are to be found in greatest numbers in Montana, Wyoming, Colorado, California, and the Dakotas, with considerable representation in Nebraska, Texas, New Mexico, Nevada, Utah, Oregon, and Idaho. Alberta and Saskatchewan, in Canada, have a few scattered remnants and they spill over into Old Mexico at the other end of their range, with the state of Kansas still maintaining a little seed stock.

It seems strange that so many of the major game animals of the new world should have been misnamed. Even the bison was erroneously called the buffalo. The pronghorn antelope suffered worst in respect to the name it was given, unless the mountain goat, which is the only North American representative of the antelope family, fared still worse. The so-called pronghorn antelope is not an antelope and has no

living kin anywhere in the world. In a sense it is just a
maverick of creation.

The antelope's feet have only two hoofs to the foot rather
than the conventional four. Unlike the deer, this animal has
a gall bladder. Its eyesight is probably as keen as that of
the mountain sheep and its sense of smell is very acute. The

Pronghorn antelope.

average mature male will not weigh more than 125 to 140
pounds. Instead of jumping fences, pronghorns usually crawl
between the wires. In the severest stormy weather they
occasionally go long distances to find shelter among bluffs
or even in the fringes of timber.

The hair of the pronghorn is quite similar to that of the
deer family. The skin is almost worthless for leather; the
flesh is rated by some as the least palatable of North American

big game animals, and by others as one of the choicest of our game meats. The truth is that a young antelope killed in its prime is meat fit for any table, but an old buck killed at the close of the rut when he is in poor condition is anything but choice meat.

To one not accustomed to seeing them, the head of the pronghorn has a weird, deformed appearance with the horns set directly above the eyes. Even the nose and face appear distorted, and the ears seem to set where they don't belong. But of all animals on the continent, pronghorns are the fleetest. They have been clocked many times at 60 and 65 miles per hour, and a few of them have done 70 miles for short distances. I have had them race my car at 50 miles per hour, outrun it and cross ahead of it at a distance of 75 or 100 yards or more. This seems to be a favorite pastime. Apparently there is an irresistible urge to demonstrate that they are the "fastest things on wheels." The habit is often taken advantage of in hunting them.

In observing a band of antelope at a distance, the most conspicuous thing about them is the white rump patch from which they can flash light by erecting the hairs. It appears to be used as a danger signal as well as a means of identification at long distances.

One of the most peculiar characteristics of the pronghorn is that although he has a hollow horn sheath, he sheds it annually. This fact was the subject of controversy for many years because the males were never seen without some kind of horns. Actually, the bone core of the antelope's horn is the only horn he has during the late fall and early winter, because he sheds the sheath rather early in the fall. The bone core is 6 to 8 inches long and is always covered with skin and fine hairs, and it is never branched. The material of which the outer horn is composed is exuded from the skin covering the bone core and is rather flexible and rubbery in its immature stage. It is apparently composed of blood and hair, together with a glutinous substance functioning as an additional binding material.

It is the outer horn alone that develops the forward extending prong from which the animal gets its name. The females frequently have horns from 2 to 4 inches long, but seldom if ever branched. After the horns are shed they disintegrate in a few months; this fact accounts for their seldom being picked up even on ranges occupied by thousands of the animals.

Pronghorn antelopes may be thought of as 100 per cent grazers; however, this is not strictly the case, for much of the short prairie vegetation that they consume cannot be classified as grass. Low-growing shrubs and weeds make up a considerable part of their diet, and I have seen old bucks going from cactus to cactus eating the flowers from the tops of the plants. They also eat both the flowers and the green seed-pods from the yucca stems. In some areas they browse on sage and greasewood. In agricultural areas they have been known to do considerable damage to both corn and kaffir corn after the grain has ripened.

Under favorable circumstances herds of antelope increase quite rapidly, since most of the mature females usually produce twins. Throughout practically their entire range the poacher has been their worst enemy, although exceptionally hard winters when deep snow covered the vegetation for long periods of time have almost wiped out complete herds. With adequate management and protection from the poacher, the pronghorn supplies an almost unbelievably large annual crop in terms of basic numbers, for legitimate hunters.

With the foregoing as a background for the understanding of pronghorn antelopes and their habits, we can better appreciate the problems associated with hunting them. Judged by almost any standard they are easier to hunt than almost any of our other big game animals, with the exception of the barren ground caribou. In areas where they are plentiful, the average hunter success-ratio is about 70 per cent. This means that nearly three out of every four men can reasonably expect to "bring home the bacon" even in a type of hunting where the average party hunts only two or three days.

The most important thing is to ascertain the general limits of a herd's range. Usually, except as they may be driven by intensive hunting or severe storms, they will cling to a range of not over 8 or 10 miles in diameter. On account of their prominent white rump patch they are easy to distinguish at long distances. The type of country they inhabit further assists in locating them, for vegetation sufficient to conceal them is unusual.

There are many methods of approach in hunting the pronghorn. The early settlers usually did it the easy way. They merely approached unobserved to within a mile or so, selected a convenient place to hide, then waved a handkerchief, a piece of cloth, or some other convenient object tied to the end of a rifle barrel, and waited for the pronghorn's natural curiosity to bring them within range. This will still work where they are not hunted too much. I have photographed them extensively and have found their curiosity the greatest aid in bringing them within the range of the camera.

I recall that one day, after spending hours trying to approach a herd of 54 head without being able to get closer than a mile, I finally parked the car and followed a draw, out of sight and on foot, until I reached the crest of the highest point of ground in the vicinity. Without exposing myself to view, I raised the camera on the tripod, above the horizon. It was not long before I heard the antelope approaching on the run. I risked a peek through the grass on top of the ridge. In a moment they stopped and ran back as fast as they had come. I took advantage of the change to ease myself up behind the tripod. In a few seconds they stopped, turned toward the camera and stared for probably a full minute; then they rapidly came forward again. For fully twenty minutes they kept up this alternate advancing and retreating, each time coming a little closer. Eventually they came within 50 yards or less before concluding that I might be dangerous, and lost no time in putting a couple of miles between us. A deer or an elk would have worked around me at a safe distance until he could determine my identity by the use of his nose; but the pronghorn, like the sheep and the goat, prefers to trust his eyes.

In some localities—and this applies particularly to areas where there is little succulent feed of any kind—the antelope frequent established water-holes at regular intervals and thus offer the hunter an opportunity to intercept them as they come and go. In other localities the animals may never go to water but depend entirely upon the vegetation to supply their needs, which are very small. In some desert areas they are known to rely upon the newer cactus growth with spines that have not yet hardened, for practically their entire supply of water.

Some hunters depend entirely upon stalking the animals, especially over terrain that is uneven or rolling. The sportsman who uses this method must be certain that he never exposes himself for a moment. If he does, the pronghorn's keen eyes are sure to discover him, in which case the best strategy is to go and hunt up an entirely different band of antelope that hasn't been disturbed.

Another favorite method is for a group on horseback to surround a herd of antelope and advance from all directions at the same time. Approached in this way, the herd will often do a lot of milling around before making up their minds what to do, and will frequently break up and dash for safety in several different directions, thus providing the hunters with a lot of shooting. I have engaged in rounding up antelope in connection with trapping and transplanting operations, and can testify that this type of hunting will prove exhilarating sport where it is not forbidden by law.

When the law does not prohibit the practice, the easiest and quickest way to get antelope is to drive an automobile load of hunters out on their range (in many places a car can go almost anywhere on the antelope range), locate a herd, and take a course parallel to them when they start to run. Almost invariably, they will swing in toward the car and attempt to cross ahead of it. This is the time to put on the brakes, roll out, and try your hand at making connections between your bullets and "streaks of greased lightning." Eventually you will learn the trick, but the novice will usually waste several boxes of shells before getting his first antelope—at least the one he is aiming at. As might be expected, this practice is being legislated against in an increasing number of states.

Where large numbers of hunters are in the field, they will keep the antelope almost constantly on the move. The longer the season continues, the more will the large bands be scattered into little bunches or even single animals that are likely to run into a lucky hunter almost anywhere.

Because of the pronghorn's way of living on the range and his high speed in traveling, a rifle in the 2,000 foot second velocity class is woefully inadequate. The antelope hunter should select a rifle of the 3,000-foot class and then confine his ammunition to the lightest weight bullet with which the shell is regularly loaded. Don't use the .22-caliber varminter, since its bullets are entirely too light to insure adequate penetration even on antelope. The lightest bullet that should ever be used on them is the 87-grain, .250–3000 Savage and .257 Roberts, using 87-grain bullets, and the .270 Winchester with the 100-grain bullet. The .300 Savage and

.30–06 with 150-grain bullets are excellent for antelope but are unnecessarily powerful. High speed and flat trajectories are the major requirements in a rifle for the pronghorn, which is likely to be shot at long range or running as nothing else on four legs can run.

CHAPTER XX

The Rocky Mountain Goat

THE Rocky Mountain goat has been called a buffalo, a sheep, an antelope, and a goat. His closest relative is the true antelope. As is the case with so many other North American animals, the misnomer has stuck with him. He has a thick undercoat of fine wool from 3 to 4 inches long, as fine as the best merino wool, although his shaggy outer coat is of long hair.

His feet are equipped with four hoofs apiece, like the majority of the world's horned animals, and he has a beard under his chin that gives him a goaty appearance. His color is pure white the year round, except for his hoofs and horns and an oily gland back of the horns, which are all black, and his eyes, which are yellow in the mature animal.

Of all the world's hoofed animals the Rocky Mountain goat is conceded to be the most sure-footed. He will even go places where the wolf and the lion cannot follow. The lion is his principal enemy and probably the only one besides man that mature goats fear to any great extent, although wolves in packs may occasionally kill them. Very young kids are preyed upon by eagles, lynxes, coyotes, wolves, and wolverines when they can be separated from their mothers.

Nature has equipped this animal with two extremely sharp daggers and dexterity in using them, so that it is probably the best able to defend itself in lone combat of all North American hoofed animals. When working alone, the best dog or wolf will be killed by one in a fair encounter, and it is probable that even the mountain lion would not attack one on the alert. In his native habitat, standing on a narrow ledge of rock on the side of a steep cliff, he is more than a match for any animal on earth. Unlike most of our big game animals, the goat is a courageous fighter and chooses to turn

Rocky mountain goat.

and fight rather than run. The mother will consistently defend her young against any intruder.

Many persons consider the Rocky Mountain goat to be monogamous. If it is not entirely so, at least it is more nearly monogamous than any of our other big game animals. Because its home is in only the highest and roughest mountain country, often above timber-line, its habits have been studied less than those of other game animals. The females are known to produce twins occasionally, but little seems to be known about the proportion that bears twins. The nanny as well as the billy has horns. In length and sharpness there is very little difference between the horns of the two sexes, but those of the females are not so large at the base. The length of horn in mature animals will run from 8 to 12 inches or a little more. The head of either sex is considered satisfactory as a trophy. In fact, the longest horns on record came from a female.

There is probably less average difference in size between the male and female goat than in any of our other species of hoofed game, excepting the peccary. A 300-pound billy is a very large animal in most parts of its range; but an exceptionally large, fat specimen is credited with weighing just over 500 pounds. On an average the male may be considered as weighing under 250 pounds, and the female under 200 pounds. In the fall of the year they are likely to carry 2 or 3 inches of fat on the back and rump.

The flesh of the goat is generally conceded to be the least palatable of all North American game species, with the single exception of the musk-ox; although during the late summer and early fall the kids and yearlings are considered fit for human consumption. Some even say they make good eating.

The skin of this inhabitant of the highest mountain peaks, where wind and storm hold sway for most of the year, is both thick and tough; but the long shaggy coat has not found a place in modern economy, although the natives of the North used to make exceptionally fine and durable blankets from its wool.

The Rocky Mountain goat is the one animal upon which civilization has made very little impression, either in the extent of its range or in its numbers. He may still be found in practically every place he was living when the first white man came (and in some places not originally inhabited). His numbers are generally considered to be as great as at any time in history, although actual estimates of the populations vary greatly. Seton made a guess that there might be 1,000,000

head of them on the North American continent, whereas
Colonel Townsend Whelen, writing in the May 1945 number of *Sports Afield*, says 75,000 to 100,000. Whelen's estimates credit Montana with 7,600; South Dakota with 200
(these were introduced by man far beyond the primitive
range); parks (other than Glacier) and grazing districts
and Indian reservations not included in above figures, with
2,804 head—totaling 19,704 head for the United States proper.
In regard to Canada and Alaska, Whelen admits that no one
knows what the actual numbers may be, although he has
attempted a feeble estimate. It should be evident that plenty
of goats still remain for those who have the hardihood to hunt
them. Whelen's estimate is that not more than 100 head
were killed by hunters in 1942, and my guess is that the kill
since 1942 to the present writing has fallen off at least 50
per cent. A lot of them must be dying annually of old age.

The Rocky Mountain goat is the least excitable of all so-
called game animals. Even when surprised, he doesn't get excited. When danger threatens he either faces it and fights or
makes his get-away if he can, without apparent haste and with
an air of independent dignity. Of all the animals I can think
of, only the skunk appears as well poised in retreat. When
he decides to leave, he seems to know where he wants to go
and takes the shortest feasible route to get there. Even when
bullets are flying all around him, he doesn't lose his head and
bolt, but watches every step he takes. If not brought down, he
will soon be where it is mighty hard for a man to follow.

Among themselves these goats are not generally quarrel-
some, and each one seems to make it a point to tend to his own
business. If they do fight, it is likely to be serious business,
and they may kill each other with the sharp stilettos with
which they are armed.

Aside from the introduced group in the Black Hills of South
Dakota, the range of the goat is confined to the Rocky Moun-

tains (including the Cabinet Range) from Montana and Idaho into Alaska, and the Cascades and coastal ranges from Washington to Cook Inlet in Alaska. Over this vast territory they are found almost exclusively in the roughest country above timber-line. They prefer the rockiest and steepest cliffs and rockslides, far above the normal range of the mountain sheep; and in summer they feed down into the small alpine meadow pockets below the cliffs. Here their range sometimes overlaps that of the sheep and the mountain caribou. Instead of coming lower in winter they work higher to the loftiest windswept ridges where a sparse vegetation seems to meet their needs.

The only exception I know to this range above timberline is along the coast of southeastern Alaska. Here I have sometimes seen goats on the cliffs along the inside passage, where considerable timbered country extends above them in places. In the sheer cliffs the goat will follow a ledge not more than 10 or 12 inches wide where even a mountain sheep could not go.

On account of the type of coat they wear, goats are very sensitive to rain, and invariably have "sense enough to go in out of the rain" under some shelter that they use as a regular retreat. Ordinarily they do not wander far from their home locality. It has been estimated that an individual seldom travels a range of more than 4 or 5 miles in any direction; but a good part of that distance may be almost straight up and straight down.

Only those who are physically hardy and willing to undergo extreme hardship and take long risks with life and limb should hunt the Rocky Mountain goat. It frequently means spending not only days, but nights as well, on bleak, windswept mountain-sides without shelter. Unlike the hunting of most species of North American big game, there is little to be said in regard to the technique of hunting this hardy denizen of the stormswept heights. The sportsman should have a good pair of binoculars with which to locate the animals and study the heads from the standpoint of their desirability as trophies. The rest is just hard work and common sense in getting within range without being seen, remembering that the animal has good eyesight. He pays little attention to noises and apparently depends on his nose for information to a much less degree than most animals.

The proper rifle for goat hunting is one with flat trajectory and adequate shocking power. Two of the best are the .270 Winchester and the .30–06. I would recommend the 130-grain bullet in the .270 and the 150-grain bullet in the .30–06. The .257 Roberts and .250–3000 Savage are also favorites with goat hunters. Since distances are likely to be great and the basis for estimating them accurately more difficult than in almost any other type of terrain, the cartridges of the 2,000-foot-velocity class are likely to be very disappointing. This is true even of those of adequate shocking power because of the grave danger of undershooting or overshooting through errors in judging distances with sufficient accuracy.

CHAPTER XXI

The Bighorn Sheep

In recent years I have spent a great deal of time following, studying, and photographing the bighorn sheep. By most sportsmen they are considered both the hardest to hunt and the most prized trophy of the North American continent. In my opinion the difficulty of hunting them has been considerably exaggerated, except for the fact that in most places it requires a rugged constitution to get into their range and to do the climbing necessary to locate them.

The bighorn's range is much more extensive than most people imagine, although much of it is closed to hunting at the present time or open only for a very limited number of licenses annually. Actually the sheep is still to be found over most of its primitive range from Lower California and well into Old Mexico to about the 68th degree of north latitude, which is very close to the Arctic Ocean at the northern extremity of Alaska. Generally speaking, the range extends east and west from the Rocky Mountains to the Cascades, and in the higher latitudes comes down almost to the sea wherever the terrain is mountainous and suited to use.

What has been said of the bighorn's range is not intended to imply that they occupy as many acres or as many square miles as they once did, but that the outside boundaries have not greatly changed. The thing that settlement has done to the bighorn is to force him off the lower districts that he once used either as winter pasture or as year-round habitat.

In the United States proper he has become a denizen of the high altitudes almost exclusively, except where cliffs and rough terrain of comparatively low altitude are so difficult of access as to be seldom visited by man. An outstanding example of this is the 3,000-foot-deep canyon of the Gunnison River in Colorado, which is so inaccessible that probably not

Rocky Mountain Bighorns. Two rams and a ewe.

more than a half dozen parties have ever traversed it. In many places the cliffs are almost perpendicular for 1,000 to 2,000 feet, with only here and there a place where even a mountain sheep could get out. It is impossible for man to hunt the area, except from the rim, for there is no possibility of getting his quarry out. Considerable of this canyon is now included within the Black Canyon National Monument, and the level of the river is lower in altitude than most of the plains and valleys of the state. The sheep population in the canyon probably remains about the same as in primitive times.

Now they seldom venture above the rims, as they did before the white man came. Other instances of the kind are to be found in rough desert areas.

As a general thing it can be said that the bighorns now cling to ranges above timber-line during both winter and summer, seeking the high windswept ridges when snow gets too deep. Just at the upper edge of timber is a favorite location during the summer months. Here small well-watered alpine meadows lie close in to rockslides and steep cliffs where they can readily take refuge in case of danger. I have seen bands of considerable size come down to the stream to drink regularly at the same place daily, and sometimes twice a day— early in the morning and late in the evening. During the summer months they go to salt licks at least two or three times a month, even though they may have to travel a considerable distance. It is probable that where they do not have access to alkali flats they do not inhabit a range entirely removed from some type of salt deposits. In country where domestic livestock is being run, the bighorns have come to depend upon the salt put out for them. This craving for salt at frequent intervals was a major contributing factor in bringing the wild sheep to near extinction in many districts during and after the market-hunting period. The hunter who could not or would not have sacrificed the time and effort to go back into the almost impenetrable cliffs for them, found it easy to hide near a salt lick and practically wipe out an entire herd in a few minutes.

In the primitive areas of the North many of the bighorn flocks may still be found in comparatively low country, provided there are rocky cliffs to furnish security from natural enemies and open meadows to feed in. The mountain sheep definitely is not an animal of the timbered areas but may move through timbered belts of some extent in going from one part to another of his customary range.

Of all big game animals the bighorn probably clings most consistently to his home range in the face of adversity and even intensive hunting. When he is pursued he inevitably comes right back to the general vicinity of the starting place. The average bighorn may live his entire life and die within 4 or 5 miles of the place where he was born; but he undoubtedly knows every trail and place to hide and how to elude a pursuer over every square foot of his home district. If driven away, he will come back as soon as it seems safe to do so. I do know, however, of some flocks that move as much as 15 or 20 miles down a canyon between their summer and winter ranges, but this is the exception rather than the general rule.

Of all the big game animals of my acquaintance I believe bighorns depend least upon nose for information. In stalking them, I have come to the conclusion that one can practically ignore the matter of wind direction except insofar as it may carry the sound of one's approach. I recall once walking up to within 12 or 15 feet of seven of them that knew I was in the vicinity but could not see the course of my approach, even though I had to walk almost directly downwind toward them. I am also sure that they are less likely to be disturbed by the noise of rolling stones and breaking twigs than any members of the deer family.

Probably the most remarkable thing about the bighorn is his sure-footedness. Unlike the goat, the bighorn bounds and jumps instead of depending on a dogged-sure-footed climb. Most of his trails take a comparatively straight, diagonal course to where he wants to go. But when he is surprised he gets away and over just as fast as he can go, and usually the "over" is almost literally straight up and over—just one high leap after another.

I once watched an old ram that I nearly stepped on while he was taking an afternoon siesta under a rock I had climbed upon in my rubber-soled shoes. He bounded up and over a series of sheer, perpendicular ledges about 6 feet in height, with the soaring sensation of an eagle rising abruptly on a strong up-current of air. He cleared one ledge that was approximately 7 feet high from a standing position on a narrow

Bighorn ram crossing open country between two rocky cliffs.

ledge, and landed squarely on all four feet drawn closely together.

The most remarkable feat I ever saw was a band of bighorns coming down over a cliff about 150 feet high. The cliff was not more than ten or fifteen degrees less than perpendicular, and the sheep were not being pursued. Apparently they had decided that that was the shortest way to where they wanted to go. An old ewe took the lead and the others followed. It looked as if it would result in certain death, but instead of leaping out into space, they kept as close to the cliff as possible, striking it every 15 or 20 feet to break the fall.

When observed closely, none of these cliffs are found to be perfectly smooth, and apparently they provide adequate projections for the sheep to use in putting on the brakes. This is also made possible by the bottoms of the bighorn's feet being equipped with thick, rough, rubbery pads with tremendous anti-skid qualities. I have seen them crossing ice that a deer would be absolutely helpless on.

Only once have I observed a sheep slip and lose its footing. In this instance a large ram jumped a chasm which appeared to be 12 or 15 feet wide, and the rocks gave away under his hind feet. He managed to throw his weight forward onto his knees, and with a convulsive kick with his hind feet against the almost perpendicular wall below, brought his rear end high enough to get his hind feet over the rim and thus lurch forward to safety. It is reported that on rare occasions they have been known to miss their footing and fall to their death.

Except during the rut, the old rams are seldom seen with the other members of the flocks. They are to be found in small bands of from three or four to fifteen or more in secluded spots where there is plenty of feed and little danger of being disturbed. Their range frequently may be at lower altitudes than that of the other mixed bands.

About the middle of September they begin to associate with the larger groups and usually remain with them until late December, after the breeding season is over. During that time they stage many a royal battle. As they clash head-on at full speed, the impact can often be heard for a mile or two. The ends of horns are frequently broken off and therefore few old rams have perfect points. When the end of the horn grows far enough around to interfere with the field of vision, they may break the ends deliberately.

The sheep, unlike most other species of big game animals, are day feeders and remain bedded down during the night. Usually the day is spent alternately feeding and lying down chewing the cud or cat-napping. At least one animal will always be on guard from some point of vantage. For this reason the sheep are extremely difficult to approach, since they have the keenest eyesight of all big game animals.

At night the bighorns usually retire to a regular bed-ground on high rock ledges that are frequently protected by over-hanging cliffs. Where shallow caves are to be found in the sides of cliffs they are often used as bedding areas. The depth of dung on regular bedding sites is proof of how long they have been used. I am convinced that the individual sheep often has his private bed-space to which he retires nightly. It will be completely rimmed around with dung until the sides may be 4 or 5 inches higher than the center, giving the appearance of the "form" occupied by a giant rabbit.

The regular night bedding-grounds are generally so situated that they are difficult of approach by coyotes, wolves, and other predators, and can be easily defended. It should be borne in mind that even a wolf is no match for an old ewe with 8- or 10-inch horns guarding a narrow ledge of rock. The mountain lion is the greatest enemy of the grown sheep, and he depends upon stealth for his success. It is not a common thing for one to overtake a sheep and kill it in its rocky retreat.

A ram with a 3-foot length of horn, measured on the outer curve, has a large head; but there are a number on record of more than 4 feet. Base circumference measurements of good heads will run from 15 to 18 inches. The horns of the white sheep of the North are more slender for their length than those of the Rocky Mountain bighorn farther south.

The mountain sheep, like so many other species of wild animals, have been arbitrarily divided into many species and subspecies. There is a gradation in color and other characteristics from the pure white sheep of the far north to the darkest sheep of the southern part of the range but their habits, in general, are not essentially different. Principal variations are mostly a matter of size and color. Whereas an average white ram will weigh around 200 pounds, an average among the

White mountain sheep from Alaska.

largest of the Rocky Mountain bighorns may go as high as 250 to 300 pounds, with individuals much larger.

Apparently all these sheep prefer grass as a diet if the supply on the particular range is adequate. Otherwise, they eat sedge, weeds of all kinds, ferns, lichens, and even browse. On their desert range they even resort to eating cactus to take the place of water, which they may never see for periods of from five to seven months at a time. In feeding on cactus they first snip the spines off with their teeth and then feed on the water-logged body of the plant. A recent study in

Wyoming indicated that the bighorns of the area were eating about 85 per cent of grasses and 15 per cent of other types of vegetation.

As far as hunting methods are concerned, there is little that can be said that would apply to one so-called species and not to another. Methods must be adapted to the terrain and to local conditions. Most bighorn hunters depend upon guides with pack outfits to get them into sheep country and get them out again, for these animals are hard to find if one depends on free lancing. The local guides should know the range of individual herds so well that the matter of finding them is not a great problem. A good pair of field glasses is almost a necessity in sheep hunting, because the important thing is either to see the sheep before they see you or to locate them from such a distance that they don't consider you a potential enemy; and this means at least 2 or 3 miles. From then on it is usually a matter of planning a successful stalk to within rifle range. This involves keeping out of sight at all times. If it is a question of going down-wind or keeping out of sight, choose the down-wind course. If you can plan to have the wind in your favor, so much the better.

Frequently bighorns are discovered in situations where it is practically impossible to approach within effective shooting range from any direction without disturbing them. By taking advantage of the sheep's instinct to flee to higher and rougher ground when frightened, success often may be achieved by working above them to some likely crossing place while another member of the party remains below and approaches from that direction. He also may get a shot under favorable circumstances. If the hunters who have gone to higher ground have used good judgment, they will almost always be rewarded if they remain quiet and concealed.

Another good means of hunting is to locate the meadows upon which rams are feeding and to approach them during the night, taking up concealed stations before the quarry leave their beds in the cliffs above. I have done this very successfully in photographing them. This method has the advantage of being easy, but the hunter must have patience and keep out of sight. Some hunt by waiting at favorable watering-places or salt licks, as the early settlers and meat hunters

Desert Bighorn sheep.

used to do. However, even though legal, none of these methods constitutes a very high order of sportsmanship.

For the man who would play the game of bighorn hunting with all the cards on the table, there is no sport more thrilling than stalking old rams on their feeding-grounds by creeping from rock to rock or from tree to tree or bush to bush, realizing that he must outwit one of the keenest sentinels in the world.

Some prefer to still-hunt the mountain sheep in his own

rocky fastness in the high mountain cliffs. The hunter who chooses this method must accept the hardships of tedious climbs and treacherous terrain; but he may be rewarded by coming face to face with a big ram around the corner of a rocky ledge. Or as I did, he may have one jump from under an overhanging rock only a few feet below him. For sheer thrills, this way of hunting the bighorn has no equal for sport in any other type of hunting anywhere in the world.

The rifle for hunting the bighorn should be one of flat trajectory as a first consideration, since distances will often be great and the terrain such that an accurate estimate of distances is extremely difficult. The .270 Winchester may be considered as the number one cartridge for sheep, using either the 100-grain or the 130-grain bullets. My personal choice would be the 100-grain bullet with 1,500 foot pounds energy, and only 4.5 inches mid-range trajectory at 300 yards.

The .250–3000 and .257 Roberts with 87-grain bullets and mid-range trajectories of only 6 inches at 300 yards, and the .30–06 with 150-grain bullet and mid-range trajectory of 6.5 inches at 300 yards are also excellent sheep rifles. The .300 H & H Magnum with the 180-grain boattails bullet has a mid-range trajectory of only 5.3 inches at 300 yards, but is unnecessarily powerful for game the size of sheep.

Owing to the long range at which sheep are frequently killed, most hunters choose to aim for the chest cavity where possible, rather than risk neck or head shots, which must depend for their effectiveness on actually breaking the spine or entering the brain. Few men can place bullets regularly into targets of this size at long range, especially under field conditions.

For hunting the bighorn and mountain goat, a telescope sight is a justifiable adjunct to the hunter's rifle, although I consider it more of a nuisance than an asset for most types of big game hunting.

CHAPTER XXII

The Musk-Ox

THE musk-ox and the American bison are very close relatives, and in many respects their habits are similar. Both are plains animals. In primitive times their ranges were very nearly equal in extent. Estimates of 50,000,000 bison far exceed the number of musk-oxen that could possibly have shared the arctic ranges with the caribou. Their number probably never exceeded from 1,000,000 to 2,000,000 head. At one time they also overran Europe and Asia. Unlike the bison, they are not and probably never were extreme migrators.

Many believe that the musk-ox is rapidly headed for extinction along with the dodo and the heath hen. There may still be a few musk-oxen in Alaska, but if so their numbers are extremely small. For generations whaling crews have shamelessly slaughtered them along the coastal regions. Explorers, adventurers, prospectors, hunters, and Indians (since the Indian has been equipped with firearms) have wantonly killed them for their skins, and even for the lust of killing. Because of their habit of turning to engage in defense combat instead of running, whole herds are easily exterminated at a single stand. Naturally, the men who have been responsible for the slaughter have not been sportsmen.

At present the musk-ox inhabits only a little fringe of Greenland and the most remote and inaccessible regions of the interior of arctic North America, together with some of the bleak islands in the Arctic Ocean. If better protective

145

laws are not passed and rigidly enforced before the airplane comes into general use by northern hunters, this noble animal is certainly doomed.

Although the musk-ox will eat almost any vegetation he can find when snow is deep and food is scarce, he is by choice a grass eater. Willows and other brush suffice to tide him

Musk-ox bull.

through the tough periods when nothing else is available. He is well equipped to dig his living from under deep snow when circumstances are not too unfavorable. For this purpose he uses feet, horns, and muzzle.

As a special adaptation to the rigors of the far north the musk-ox is supplied with a heavy coat of brown wool underneath a coat of hair from 12 to 20 inches long, reaching down so far as to give him the appearance of being almost rectangular in shape, and heavier than he actually is. A large bull will ordinarily weigh 600 or 700 pounds. If not a record weight, one of 900 pounds may be considered very nearly as large as any ever gets. In the fall these animals are likely to be extremely fat.

The horns of the musk-ox form a shield on top of the head, turning down along the sides of the face and up at the ends to form sharp and formidable hooks. For all practical purposes the tail is non-existent. Hoofs are broad and rounded on the toes, making an almost round track. The animal is capable of exuding a very strong musky odor, from which it derives its name.

Ordinarily the flesh of the musk-ox is so strongly flavored with musk as to be unacceptable as food for the white man. Some claim that the animal may be handled and dressed in such a way as to eliminate the objectionable flavor almost entirely. In the early days some northern tribes depended almost exclusively upon these animals for food, clothing, and shelter, as well as for the materials from which to make implements of all kinds.

Hunting the musk-ox, like hunting the barren ground caribou, can scarcely be classified as sport. Northern natives generally used dogs to bring their quarry to bay for the slaughter. In defending themselves they make a mass formation with heads facing out. The mature bulls take positions on the outside of the mass and charge at the enemy when too closely pressed, although usually only one bull charges at a time. The cows and calves are given protection on the inner side of the circle. When they are brought to bay, the hunter may approach as close as he considers safe and select shots to his own choosing. Where dogs are not used, it sometimes requires a lot of trailing to get within shooting range of a herd. They are seldom found alone at any time of year, but may occasionally be found in pairs. To locate a herd of musk-oxen today may require weeks or even months of searching over a vast arctic waste, unless an airplane is resorted to.

There is no great advantage in the newer high-velocity rifles in hunting the musk-ox. The .30–30, .30–40, .35 Remington, .35 Winchester, 8 mm Mauser are all more than adequate under usual conditions. The .30–06 is an ideal rifle because of its range of bullet weights. Not many of our readers will ever see a musk-ox in its native haunts; hence such a chapter as this is almost superfluous, except for giving the sportsman a broader knowledge of one of North America's little-known game animals.

CHAPTER XXIII

The Black Bear

The black bear is the most universally distributed big game animal on the North American continent. It is true that he is not to be found in great abundance throughout much of his range; but the remarkable thing is that he still persists at all, in spite of the encroachments of civilization and the bad name that has followed him since the earliest days.

In spite of all that has been said and written to the contrary, the black bear is a very peaceful animal. Instead of the bloodthirsty stock killer that he is frequently pictured to be, he is primarily a vegetarian and an eater of insects, small rodents, and carrion. The bear that will kill anything larger than a woodchuck for food is exceptional rather than usual. Occasionally one does get a taste for the warm blood of domestic livestock and becomes a killer; but these exceptions are very few.

The common black bear is subject to many variations in color and size and is credited with a variety of subspecies. Color phases vary from extremely light buff to coal-black. Cubs of different color are found frequently in the same litter. Two cubs to the litter is the rule, but three are not uncommon. The so-called cinnamon bear, as well as the glacier bear of the North, are both members in good standing of the black bear family. Many bears that are otherwise all black have a white marking on the throat or chest.

In the northern part of his range (and he is found from

149

almost the northern limits of timber well into Central America), he goes into hibernation when the weather gets cold enough to cut off the major portion of his customary food supply, or when the snow begins to lie on the ground permanently. Throughout the Rockies of the United States few are active after the middle of December. In winters of deep,

The common black bear of North America.

early snows they may den up as early as the first of November, or even earlier in the higher altitudes.

I have seen their tracks in a foot of snow in northern Montana as late as December 22nd. They come out of hibernation when most of the snow has melted off in the spring. The young are born in the winter dens, which may be in a cave in the rocks, under heavy windfall, under the trunk of a large tree upturned by the roots, or even under the overhanging boughs of a great spruce tree where the snow will soon seal them in.

The first food taken in early spring is invariably coarse vegetation, such as bear grass, elk grass or other plants that get green early. There is also good evidence that for a week or two before going into hibernation they eat only coarse vegetation, and very little of that at the last. Nature apparently thus provides for the animal's alimentary tract being properly conditioned for the long period of inactivity.

The black bear is very fond of ants and their larvae, of beetles, bees and honey. Rodents form a considerable part of his regular diet, and fruits and vegetables are favorite foods whenever he can find them. At times he will catch fish in shallow water, and is very fond of them.

One of the most conspicuous bear signs is turned-over stones on hillsides where an animal has been working for ants, beetles, and other insects. The strong-smelling, semi-decayed carcasses of sheep, cattle, horses, and big game animals are always attractive to the black bear's appetite. Where bears are hunted in the spring this weakness for carrion is often Bruin's undoing.

The pelt of the bear is of little value except as an ornament for wall or floor. The hair is at its best late in the fall or soon after the animal emerges from hibernation. Later in the spring the pelt is likely to be faded and rubbed. Early in the fall it is short and not fully prime.

The flesh of the black bear is very palatable, especially in the fall when the animals are feeding on berries. I prefer young bear steaks to venison. Old males may be somewhat strong. The fat of the bear is one of the finest cooking oils known. I used to sell it regularly to bakers of pastries for double the price of hog-fat. One should save all the fat from the entrails as well as from other parts of the carcass. As far as the quality of the fat is concerned, I have never been able to see any difference between that from a cub and an old male, except that the old male has more of it. I have taken as much as 50 pounds of pure oil from a single animal. The fat should be "tried out" exactly like that from a hog.

The hind quarters of the black bear may be sugar-cured and smoked like pork, using the same formula. When living

Black bear in tree.

on the Montana ranch I occasionally used to send a sugar-cured bear quarter to my father, who lived in Iowa. He was extremely fond of it. Most of his friends who ate it never knew that it was not first-class pork ham.

If you have any finicky people around, be sure to cut the feet off the carcass before hanging the meat up for use. When these are skinned out, they so closely resemble human hands and feet that many sensitive people never get over the thought. My wife was very fond of bear meat until she happened to see a complete carcass hanging up in our screened-in meat safe. It reminded her so much of the human species that she has never eaten a mouthful of bear meat since.

In proportion to their numbers, bears are probably seen less frequently than any other game animal. They have learned to avoid man, and they usually confine their activities to brushy and heavily timbered areas where they are difficult to observe and where they can hear and smell their only natural enemy before he is aware of their presence. Although the bear's eyesight is comparatively poor, his keen nose and ears are usually adequate to warn him in time.

The bear is not a coward, but he is discreet. A mother with cubs will not hesitate to attack if she believes her off-spring are in danger; but given time, she will lead them out of danger or boost them up a tree and get out of the way. It is poor policy to get between a bear and her cubs. I have met them at close quarters on a number of occasions, and never had one charge; but I also used discretion and permitted the old mother bear to "save face" in the process.

I once parted the willows on a trail leading to a spring in a clump of trees that grew at the edge of a swampy meadow. A mother bear and her cubs were on a log across the spring not more than 6 feet from my face. They were apparently catching a mess of frogs for breakfast. I stood my ground for about fifteen seconds (it seemed like fifteen minutes), expecting her to yield the right-of-way. It became apparent that she was going to take the initiative in expelling me from the premises. I quietly withdrew without indicating either haste or fear. As soon as I was no longer an immediate threat, she lost no time in getting her family out of the vicinity. We both "saved face" in the process.

On another occasion I met one around a sharp curve in a bear trail through thick ferns and underbrush. We were about 10 feet apart and I stood my ground. After considerable threatening she led the way off the trail, and in a few seconds it was evident from the crashing underbrush that we would be a long way apart in very short order.

When badly wounded or cornered, the black bear will fight with no thought of fear. During the last hunting season I heard of a mortally wounded bear charging his frightened antagonist who fired an additional five shots without scoring

Medium-sized black bear killed while feeding on Kinnikinik berries in northwestern Montana.

a hit as the bear rushed in at close range. The hunter was trapped with his back to a cliff. The only circumstance that saved him was the fact that the bear fell dead at his feet from the first shot.

Two other bears shot last fall by acquaintances were reported to have charged after the first bullet found its mark. In both instances the hunters were good shots and stopped them before they got uncomfortably close. I believe that many bears credited with charging merely run toward the hunter because they mistake the direction from which the sound of the gun comes. In a canyon or against cliffs, it is often difficult for an experienced man to judge the direction of a rifle report. The last bear I shot ran from me as fast as he could go as soon as he was hit, but he saw and recognized me just as I fired. There is no hard and fast rule in regard to a bear's behavior when wounded; but the hunter should always be prepared to stop a charge.

There is a great deal of difference in the size of mature black bears. I have killed a great many and I doubt that the heaviest of them would weigh much more than 400 pounds. I have killed mature bears in the spring that would not weigh more than 150 pounds. The largest one I ever saw was in Gold Basin in Alaska. At the time, I was hunting Alaska brownies and didn't want to pack two heavy hides out over a long, hard trek. The bear, crossing a frozen muskeg, was at close range and I estimated his weight at 500 pounds.

There are authentic records of more than 600 pounds for the black bear, and one was killed by several cowboys on the Uncompahgre Mesa in Colorado some years ago that was credited with weighing 700 pounds. This animal took an unbelievable amount of lead from .30–30 rifles. Without sworn records on the weight I would be inclined to think 700 pounds an exaggeration.

Early in the spring bears may be located on snow-free slopes where lush vegetation has started to grow and where edible roots may be dug up for food. They may be spotted from tops of adjacent ridges with binoculars, and stalked until within satisfactory shooting distance. Old burns are also good places to find them seeking small rodents, or tearing rotten logs open for the ants and grubs that are frequently in them.

In the fall of the year there is no better place to locate

bears than berry and scrub-oak patches. Here, too, they are more or less off guard while feeding and can be more readily approached without being disturbed. If possible, find a prominence overlooking a hillside of berries or oak with a good crop of acorns where they regularly feed. At this time of year they are sure to be fat and their flesh is of best flavor.

Scanning likely bear country with the glasses. Ten-foot snow crest behind the hunter.

Most bears, especially in big game country, are killed as the result of the hunter's stumbling on them accidentally. In most places the open season on bears coincides with that of other species of big game, such as deer, elk, moose, sheep, and goats. The hunter should always be on the alert in order to locate the bear first.

There are a number of ways of hunting the black bear. The most effective method is to use dogs to tree the animal or bring it to bay where it can easily be killed. There can't be much sportsmanship in this method, and it is rapidly being outlawed in most parts of the country. Since the black bear is easily treed, the chase is usually short when the dogs once get on a fresh trail. Some states permit the use of dogs on leash in hunting bears. The principal advantage over the use of no dogs is that the hunting is less haphazard. It does not lessen the amount of skill required on the part of the hunter to locate the game before he locates you.

In the West, cattle and bears occupy the same range in many places. Cattle on the range customarily pay no attention whatever to bears in their vicinity. Only three days before this was written I took a moving picture of a very large brown bear walking through a herd of cattle that did not even look up from their feeding. In the spring of the year many cattle die from eating larkspur, and the bears invariably frequent the carcasses until they are entirely consumed. If bear hunting is permitted in the spring, the easiest way to get a specimen is to find some place where cattle have access to larkspur. Locate a carcass and wait for the bear to show up.

I killed my first black bear with a .25–35 Winchester carbine, and he never moved out of his tracks. He weighed about 250 pounds and was very fat. I have never had a bear go more than 25 or 30 feet after being hit, with the single exception of one shot with defective ammunition; and he made a clean get-away. Usually I have made it a point to place the bullet in the center of the forehead, at the base of the skull, or to break the back just over the shoulders. I have never been inclined to shoot at random at bears or any other game. A bear shot through the heart or lungs may live long enough to do a lot of damage before he takes the final count. Where one exercises judgment in placing his shots, any of the accepted deer rifles are adequate for the black bear.

For the fellow who expects to shoot merely at the bear rather than at a particular small vital area, I would suggest the .30–40, 8 mm Mauser, .348 Winchester with 250-grain bullet, .35 Winchester, .405 Winchester, .300 Savage, .30–06 or .270 Winchester. I have shot a lot of them with the .250–3000 Savage, which is a good killer in the hands of one who knows its limitations and can place his shots.

CHAPTER XXIV

The Grizzly and Alaska Brown Bears

To justify the consideration of the grizzly and Alaska brown bears together, I would point out the fact that there is no clear dividing-line between the place where the one species leaves off and the other begins. They all have common characteristics distinguishing them from other members of the bear family. All have broader heads and dished faces. All have evidence of more or less of a hump at the shoulders. All have characteristically longer and straighter claws on the front feet than do most other species of bears.

In color they range from very light grizzly gray to very dark brown, and in general their habits are quite similar—modified, of course, by the particular environment. Within this broad range of large bears there are many strains, and hair-splitting naturalists have had a Roman holiday attaching names to so-called subspecies within the group.

Some mature grizzly bears are smaller than the largest members of the black species. A very old female grizzly of an extremely light color was killed in central Colorado a couple of years ago. It was in fair condition and was estimated by a man who has weighed many bears as not heavier than 400 pounds. A good many of the old males will weigh 700 or 800 pounds; a few have actually tipped the scales at nearly 1,200 pounds. Likewise, a few of the big Alaska browns have been reported to weigh as much as 1,800 pounds.

The characteristic color of the grizzly is due to lighter-

colored tips on hairs of darker hue, and it varies greatly with
the individual bear. Apparently very old animals are likely
to have more white-tipped hairs than the younger specimens.
Some are so light as to appear almost a dingy white in color.
Others are hardly distinguished from some of the dark rusty-
brown shades of the black bear species.

Grizzly bear.

At one time the range of the grizzly extended well out
on the buffalo plains where they may have helped dispose of
sick stragglers, animals that had died from eating poison
plants, and young calves. Occasionally one may have developed into a killer of mature buffalo. This was probably
the exception rather than the rule, for few of them have developed into killers of either big game animals or domestic
livestock.

When a grizzly does run amuck he is likely to be most
destructive of livestock. I once knew one in northwestern

Montana that killed eleven three- and four-year-old steers in one large winter feed-lot in about twenty nights. The evidence indicated that he always came at night when the cattle were bedded down. Usually the steer would get up and run before the bear could make contact. Tracks in the snow indicated that the grizzly would overtake the steer in 50 to 100 yards, when he would pull up alongside and presumably strike the steer on the head with a front foot and break his neck.

One four-year-old steer was dragged about 200 yards to the top of a knoll before the bear settled down for his meal. This bear never returned to feed on a cold carcass, but killed his meat fresh every trip. A posse of ranchers finally got on his trail and lost him at night about 60 miles from the starting point. They got several long-range shots at him but apparently never drew blood. The old fellow used good judgment in never returning to the locality. He must have left the cattle country for some peaceful wilderness area, for he was never heard of again.

When the first white men came into the grizzly's domain they found the animal afraid of nothing and not disposed to give the right-of-way on a trail. He never looked for trouble but was willing to fight anything that challenged his right to go where he pleased and do as he pleased. The Indians seldom tackled him alone and, for the most part, seemed to have molested him very seldom. The Indian who killed a grizzly was the object of considerable admiration. I have found bones of grizzlies, however, in the prehistoric cave dwellings of the Southwest, associated with pre-bow-and-arrow culture, that is, with the culture of the dart throwers.

The repeating rifle has changed both the grizzly's disposition and his habits. The few that have not been exterminated have gone back into the most remote and rugged mountainous areas where man seldom penetrates. When he is in the vicinity, Mr. Grizzly usually yields the right-of-way long before the man suspects that he is anywhere near. In fact, the once monarch of the whole of Nature's realm has become timid in the presence of man, so long as he can save face in the process or is not wounded or does not consider himself cornered. The mother who believes her cubs to be in danger is certainly to be avoided.

It may be said that at the present time the grizzly is confined to the remote wilderness areas of the Rockies and the Cascades from Old Mexico and California to the limit of timber in Alaska and Canada, with one specialized type inhabiting the barrens of the north clear to the shores of the Arctic Ocean.

The tracks of the grizzly can be distinguished from those of the black bear by the length of the claw marks (sometimes 3 or 4 inches long) and by the fact that the claws of all five toes usually leave imprints, whereas the claw on the thumb of the black bear seldom leaves a mark. The front track of a large grizzly will frequently measure 6 inches wide and 8 inches long and the track of the hind foot 6½ or 7 inches wide and 12 to 14 inches long. This will compare with a hind foot track of 11 inches by 16 or 18 inches for the largest of the Alaska browns, and with 4 by 6 to 8 inches for a good-sized black bear.

Like the black bear, the average grizzly will seldom kill an animal larger than a woodchuck and is very fond of the smaller rodents such as ground squirrels, gophers, and mice. He is a great insect eater and probably depends more upon vegetable matter than does the black bear. In the spring tender grasses may constitute the bulk of the grizzly's diet, and later in the season roots, herbs, and berries are eaten. Along the salmon streams of the West, he, like the Alaska brownie, depends very largely on fish as a diet. Even in our Rockies the grizzlies frequently engage in fishing for trout to vary their meals.

The mature grizzly never climbs trees, but the cubs do. The long, straight claws of the older animals are not adapted to sinking into the bark of a tree. The adults do, however, have the habit of standing at the base of a tree, reaching as high as possible and tearing a chip out by using the teeth.

There are many frontier tales of individual grizzly bears that terrorized the ranchers for thirty or forty years. This animal may sometimes reach the age of forty years but it is safe to assume that is nearer a maximum than an average.

There is considerable support for the belief that the grizzly, like the black bear, is more likely to take up livestock killing late in life as an easier way to make a living when his faculties are slowing down. The very old female grizzly mentioned earlier in the chapter was killed at the carcass of a yearling heifer that she had apparently killed two or three days earlier. Incidentally, she had the additional handicap of having lost one front foot in a trap. The evidence showed that she had camped beside the carcass during that time, presumably to keep other meat eaters away. This grizzly was killed by one lucky shot from a .22 Savage high-power rifle which severed the main artery of the back just below the spine and caused her to bleed to death in the shortest possible time.

In the United States proper the grizzly is now to be found only in our national parks and in relatively inaccessible wilderness areas in the high mountain ranges. Some states are already offering them some satisfactory protection.

In western Canada and Alaska where hunting is less intense, the grizzly's distribution is much more general. However, this bear prefers a timbered country (excepting the arctic grizzly) and the mountain valleys and slopes near timberline where he finds a great many root plants and vegetation attractive to his taste, in addition to marmots and other rodents.

The range of an individual grizzly is likely to be considerably greater than that of the black bear species. A

radius of operations of 40 to 60 miles appears to be not uncommon, and there is no living thing that travels on four
legs within his range that does not unquestionably yield him
the right-of-way. The large mountain lion may do it grudg-
ingly, but according to all reports he knows better than to
attack the animal that might easily break his neck with one
swipe of his powerful front paw.

Hunting grizzlies with dogs has never been considered too
satisfactory. The animal cannot be treed, for the mature
grizzly can't climb, and he is not prone to come to bay. His
habit is to carry on a running fight in which the dogs are
frequently eliminated one by one along the trail. Any dog
that makes the mistake of getting within reach of either teeth
or front paws is usually eliminated on the spot. There is a
record of a 60-mile chase by a pack of good dogs in hot
pursuit; but the old grizzly was no worse for wear when
the dogs were all put out of the way by his swift, forceful
blows.

The hunting of the grizzly and the Alaska brownies is so
similar that I shall cover them together. In the meantime, some
further discussion of the big Alaska bears is in order. Much
of what has been said of the grizzly is equally true of the
big browns. Their food habits are very similar except that
the brownies depend on a fish diet to a greater extent than
most of the grizzlies. I believe, however, that where they
occupy the same range the grizzly will eat just as large a
proportion of salmon as his close cousin.

The brownie is not characterized by the gray-tipped hairs
to the extent that the average grizzly is, and his general color
is a considerably darker brown. In most specimens the
claws on the front feet are likely to be somewhat heavier
and slightly shorter than those of a grizzly of proportionate
size. The average of the mature browns is considerably
smaller than the larger of the grizzlies; but the largest speci-

mens of the Alaska browns are far larger than the largest of the big grizzlies.

Like the grizzly, the Alaskan browns attend to their own business so far as man is concerned, unless molested. A few instances of unprovoked attack have been recorded; but in most of these the bears were carrying bullets and scars from

Alaska brown bear on Admiralty Island.

previous encounters with man, as well as an unsatisfied grudge against the two-legged species. In districts where they have been hunted they give the man-scent a wide berth.

Both the brown and the grizzly den up during the winter months and usually stay in hibernation longer than the blacks. They are also generally credited with hibernating at higher altitudes than black bears.

The big brown bear is confined almost exclusively to the Pacific coastal areas of Alaska from near its southern extremity to the end of the Alaska Peninsula, including the larger islands along the coast. The strip is comparatively narrow, seldom extending far down the slope of the opposite sides of the mountains forming the coast-line. His individual range is probably as large as that of the grizzly, and he has beaten trails connecting one type of environment with another. I have followed these uninterrupted paths through devils club, brush, and across muskegs, dense forest, and open mountain-sides for 10 or 15 miles at a time.

When Mr. Brownie starts out for a new feeding-ground he seems to know in advance exactly where he plans to go. Along the tide-flats he eats a great deal of kelp and will dig for clams and other marine mollusks at low tide.

Those who would hunt either the grizzly or the big brown bears early in the spring are likely to find them associated with small mountain meadows and snowbanks near timberline or above. They frequently depend upon willow and alder patches for cover. During the summer months they are likely to be found in dense brush close to watercourses. During the salmon run, most of the Alaska members of both species will be congregated along the salmon spawning streams. After the berries ripen, the best place to look for them is in and around the densest berry patches. When the berries are gone they may be found along the tide-flats or back in the high country making preparation for hibernation.

Most hunters prefer a trophy taken in the spring soon after the animal is out of hibernation. The pelt is at its very best at this time and the bears are more easily hunted then than during the short period preceding hibernation when the fur is in acceptable condition.

Both the grizzly and Alaska brown bears should be hunted the casual way, by locating them through field glasses from prominences overlooking their favorite haunts. After they are located, the strategy of the stalk can be planned in conformity with the circumstances.

Along the Alaska coast many of the local residents locate the big bears by cruising the coast-line. When they are sighted, the landing is made far enough away that the bears will not be disturbed, and the stalk planned in accordance with circumstances.

The sportsman who hunts any species of big bear should secure a good guide and depend on him for detailed advice. In fact, most of the political jurisdictions where grizzlies and browns are to be found require that the sportsman *must* be accompanied by a guide. It is mandatory for hunting all big game in Alaska, and is increasingly a requirement in other territory. Certainly, it is the only satisfactory way to hunt such dangerous game as the large bears.

The skin of either the grizzly or the brown is a splendid trophy and makes an imposing ornament for the floor or for the wall of the den, if the ceiling is high enough to accommodate it. These skins will usually measure more than 8 feet each way. Some will measure 10 or 11 feet.

I have a friend who lived in Alaska when I was living there, who had a trapping lease up the Stikine River on one of its British Columbia tributaries not so many miles from the world-famous Cassair hunting district. One fall he built three small cabins at convenient intervals along his trap-lines to use as overnight stations. I do not know the exact dimensions of these log houses, but he told me that he roofed each of them with a single skin of a bear, tacked fur side down on the sloping rafters. I asked him what species of bear they were; he said he didn't know whether they were grizzlies or Alaska brownies, but that he had killed the bear in each case within a few hundred yards of the particular cabin where its hide was used. My friend said these bears were so numerous that one could be killed almost anywhere in that area. He may still be running that trap-line every winter, for all I know, since I have not heard from him for some time.

The big bears have been killed with all kinds of rifles from the .25–35 and the .22 Savage high power, on up. One man even tackled an Alaska brown with the .220 Swift—about the most unsatisfactory thing in the world to use on a heavy bear because the bullet disintegrates into lead vapor before it has penetrated more than the mere surface. By sheer good luck

Stikine River boat, Hazel B No. 2, leaving Wrangell, Alaska, for Telegraph Creek, British Columbia. This is the favorite route to the famous Dease Lake and Cassair hunting districts.

he lived to tell the tale and warn other varmint rifle enthusiasts never to try the same experiment if they value their lives.

I have hunted the Alaska bears with the 8 mm Mauser, using the 236-grain bullet. I would not advise the use of anything less powerful. Its energy is almost identical with that of the .30–40 using 220-grain bullet and with the .300 Savage. I would say that these and the .270 Winchester with

150-grain bullet should be considered as representing the very minimum of fire-power required for such game.

The .30–06 with 220-grain bullet represents a slight advantage over the cartridges just named; but I consider it as light for our largest members of either the grizzly or Alaska brown bear families.

My choice as the ideal cartridge for these big fellows is the .375 H & H Magnum with 300-grain bullet delivering a wallop of 4,300 foot pounds at close range, should one need it. The next best is the .300 H & H Magnum with fully 1,000 pounds less energy at the muzzle.

I have consistently contended that the heart shot is the best objective for the average hunter for most big game. For the big bears I do not recommend a heart shot unless the animal is a considerable distance away and standing broadside in such a way that the bullet will not have to crash through the heavy shoulder bones and muscles to get there. Be sure the bear is far enough away for a heart shot to be effective before he can cover the distance between himself and the hunter. This may take a minute or more, and at close range the bear might do a lot of damage before he goes down.

At close range on a broadside shot, I would recommend a bullet at the base of the ear or through the spine above the shoulders; and don't make a bum guess as to where the spine is. Early in the spring there is a lot of hair above a big bear's back, besides another 5 or 6 inches of non-vital area.

Some hunters aim to break the shoulder, but an enraged bear with one shoulder out of commission is more than a match for the average man with a gun at close quarters. If a big bear is coming straight on with his head raised to the level of his back, put your bead on the end of his nose and he will usually stop in his tracks. If his head is below the level of his back, aim for his neck directly between the ears. If his head is down feeding, a shot in the center of the forehead is probably the best; but when the head is raised, the angle of the skull is too oblique to offer any assurance that the bullet will not be deflected without penetrating the brain.

Play safe when hunting the big bears. Many sportsmen and hunters have paid with their lives for their poor judgment or carelessness.

CHAPTER XXV

The Polar Bear

THE polar bear is the most distinctive of all our bear species. This is true not only of his color but also of his general shape and build and of his habits of life. He is almost as much at home in the ocean as on land. Instead of the customary tough, calloused foot pads of other members of the bear clan, the polar bear has pads of stiff bristles which enable him to walk on slippery ice-floes without slipping.

Although the polar bear roams farther north than any other land animal, it does not hibernate except when about to produce young. This, of course, is Nature's only way of protecting such helpless, undersized creatures as bear cubs are when born, and as they remain for a good many weeks.

The range of the polar bear is the rim of the Arctic Ocean, including the edge of Hudson Bay, the shores of Greenland, and the islands lying in the Arctic Ocean. Actually, it extends farther off-shore than it does onto the land back of the beaches. Favorite haunts are the broken ice-floes of the coasts.

In general, this unique bear isn't much interested in either unbroken ice or unbroken land. His need is a place where he can put his feet on something solid while he eats what he takes from the sea, and where he can stretch out and relax for an occasional rest. The polar bear hunter should think in terms of a sturdy boat capable of poking in and out among ice-floes, in preference to a land expedition, although this too is frequently undertaken.

In common with other members of the bear family, the polar bear can subsist on vegetation, and at times of the year may depend upon grass and roots for the major part of his food. However, he is usually thought of as a fish and seal eater. It is not unlikely that the average polar bear spends a lot more time in the water and on floating ice than he does

Polar bear.

on land, for his staple items of diet come from the sea. Seals, fish, young walrus, arctic birds and their eggs, and the carcasses of dead whales washed ashore constitute the main food supply during most of the year.

The polar bear's sense of smell may be keener than that of any other animal. It is said that these animals will gather from a radius of 20 miles to feast on a carcass of a whale washed ashore, locating it apparently by scent alone. Their vision is also credited with being the best of any member of the bear family. This should be expected, in view of the animal's general habits and environment. His hearing is probably below standard, since his environment and mode of life do not require much dependence upon it.

The polar bear is extremely quick in his movements; otherwise he would not be able to catch the wary seal. In the water his usual swimming speed is about 3 miles per hour, but he is credited with being able to double this or even better for short distances. He depends upon his front legs almost entirely while swimming, and allows his hind legs to extend straight behind him.

Few white men consider the flesh of the polar bear to be fit for food, although the cubs are declared by some to be very good eating. Some say that the flesh of adults that have been feeding for some time on vegetation is relatively good eating. The general consensus of opinion is that this animal's flesh is not suitable for consumption by civilized men. I cannot speak from personal experience, for I have never tried eating it.

The fur of the young polar bear is pure white, but in many of the older specimens it has become stained to a yellowish tinge. The pelt is considered one of the finest trophies in the world for use as a floor rug.

The polar bear is larger and heavier than the public generally believes, in comparison with other bears. The average mature female will weigh about 700 pounds and the average male about 900 pounds. Individual specimens have been weighed in at more than 1,600 pounds. Some have been estimated as being even heavier. It seems certain that only the great brown bear of the North is larger than the polar bear, and that the difference is not great between extremely large specimens of the two species.

A hungry polar bear has been known to attack man without provocation; but this is the extreme exception. In general, they do not appear to be as fearful of man as the large land bears, but this is probably because they have had less contact with the fellow who carries a high-power rifle. Like the grizzly and the Alaskan brown, the polar bear is a savage fighter when wounded or cornered.

On account of his habitat this animal is not bothered with

Steamship from Seattle coming up Inside Passage loaded with hunters for the North Country, preparing to dock at Wrangell, Alaska. The Inside Passage trip is rated the most beautiful ocean trip made by any company on a regular run. "Elephant's Nose" is in the background of the picture.

weekend hunters. The man who hunts polar bears now must organize an expedition with expert guides and elaborate equipment. For this reason there is little need to go into details of hunting methods in a book of this kind. With modern high-power rifles, the most important thing is to locate the bear and to maneuver into effective shooting range. If the carcass of a whale can be located on the beach, the killing of a polar bear should be merely a matter of routine.

In the not too distant future it may be that the tables will be turned on the polar bear, and he may find himself the most consistently pursued of any member of the bear tribe; in this case extermination may be just around the corner. I refer to the use of the airplane in locating and hunting this quarry.

As these bears live in an environment where Nature has made no provision for their concealment from above, an airplane cruising along the coastal areas should offer the hunter every advantage in locating them, as well as a direct means of approach from camps located even hundreds of miles distant. I hope, for the sake of this noble and courageous animal, that in the meantime laws will be enacted to protect him from this unfair type of exploitation. I have recently visited taxidermists' shops where large numbers of polar bear skins were waiting to be made up into rugs. Invariably their history was that they had been flown in from Alaska by members of our armed forces. The tales some of these young officers tell of wholesale slaughter of these noble animals as well as other species of game by strafing or bombing from the air suggests the urgent need by our Army and Navy and Air Force officials of a much greater conservation consciousness than now exists.

As to the type of rifle for use on the polar bear, and for the most vulnerable spots on the animal, I would refer the reader to what has been said on this subject relative to the big brown and the grizzly. It is a mistake to use too light a rifle on so dangerous an animal as a polar bear.

CHAPTER XXVI

The Peccary

THIS chapter on hunting the peccary is not an afterthought. There is adequate justification for not including the peccary as a big game animal; but he gained a reputation during frontier days in the Southwest that entitles him to a place in any treatise on American game animals. I have never hunted this superb little animal, but folklore is replete with stories of his courage and his sagacity. Like the wolf and the grizzly bear, he has adjusted his habits and actions in line with the changing requirements of self-preservation.

I think that it cannot be doubted that before they were intensively hunted with firearms, groups of peccaries would not hesitate to attack man. The stories of peccaries treeing a hunter are undoubtedly well founded in fact as well as in tradition. There was also a time when the wolf and the grizzly had little respect for man's prestige; but today their greatest interest is to keep as far away from him as possible.

So it is with the peccary, insofar as his range overlaps that of man in his domestic state. When the peccary discovers man's presence he gets out of sight and away just as fast as he can. As far as I can learn, there is no exception to this rule in areas where they have been hunted to any great extent, and this certainly includes their entire range north of Central America.

The range of the peccary never extended very far north of the Mexican border. Texas is credited with a peccary population of 38,000 (1945), which is much greater than any other state above the Mexican border. A few scattered bands are still to be found in New Mexico and Arizona, but the hunter who would find them in abundance should plan to go below the southern boundary of the United States.

Although the peccary is usually thought of as a wild hog, he is in reality only distantly related to the true hog. Be-

The collared peccary.

low the border he is generally called the "javeline." In some localities he is known as the "musk hog." The latter name is derived from the fact that both sexes have a large musk gland in the middle of the rump about 7 or 8 inches forward of the bump that takes the place of a tail. A very offensive odor may be emitted from this gland at will, which may serve to keep mosquitoes away. This gland must be cut out immediately after the animal is killed if the flesh is to be used for food; otherwise the meat will be badly tainted. The flesh of young animals is considered very good; and some claim that if properly dressed and cared for, the meat of all peccaries except the old boars is desirable for food.

There is little difference in size between the two sexes. Animals that will stand from 24 to 26 inches high at the shoulders and weigh 55 to 65 pounds may be considered large, although these probably are not top figures for the species. They seldom, if ever, take on any considerable amount of fat. The familiar collared peccary, which is the northern species, appears almost black at a distance, although he has a sprinkling of tawnish or grayish hairs around the head and a narrow collar of the same color.

The lifetime range of the individual peccary herd is presumed to be very limited, provided the animals have adequate food and shelter and are not too much molested. More than any other North American hoofed animal, they depend upon natural shelter in protecting themselves from their enemies. Their beds for the night are frequently in caves in the rocks, in hollow logs or in the hollowed-out bases of standing trees. They often get temporary protection by backing into holes dug in the ground by other animals.

Like the domestic hog, the peccary roots a great deal for a living, and his range may readily be identified by the rooted-up patches of ground where he has been digging for edible bulbs and roots. Peccaries eat almost anything they can find that would tempt the appetite of other members of the hog family. They are very fond of acorns and nuts of all kinds, and they carry on depredations in cultivated fields bordering their range. They eat snakes and lizards when they can catch them.

The peccary is not confined to any single type of country and is to be found in the swampy, timbered lowlands as well as on the cactus and chaparral plains and the brush-covered rocky mountain-sides. His principal interest seems to be to have adequate food and cover.

As with other members of the wild hog family, peccaries are often hunted with dogs. Where dogs are not used, the type of hunting has to be adapted to the terrain. On rocky mountain-sides they are usually surprised while feeding during the morning or late afternoon hours, and shot while seeking cover. During midday they may be flushed from their protected lairs where they have retired for midday siestas. In chaparral and cactus they are frequently hunted from horseback.

Except where peccaries are to be met with at long range, almost any deer rifle is satisfactory. At long range one of the flat-trajectory varmint rifles is very effective. If the spoiling of a lot of meat is not a drawback, the .220 Swift will do the trick when there is no intervening brush. Where brush is very likely to interfere, the hunter should select one of the controlled expansion type of bullets such as the Winchester Silvertip. The .250–3000 Savage, .257 Roberts, and .270 Winchester are ideal rifles for hunting peccaries in comparatively open country.

CHAPTER XXVII

Record Heads and Horns

TROPHIES of the chase have been a fad with hunters ever since time immemorial. Primitive men seem to have been more interested in teeth and claws and fancy feathers than anything else as trophies. Antlers, horns, and skins were to them as useful, in many instances, as was the flesh. Besides, they had no taxidermists and no fancy dens in which to display the heads and horns in an attractive way. For a long time the civilized sportsman of Europe and America has been interested in preserving and displaying especially fine specimens of horns and antlers.

Prentiss N. Gray, a member of the Boone and Crockett Club, is credited with being the first American to realize the importance of preserving and compiling records of outstanding American big game trophies. Europe had preceded us by many years in this field.

In 1932, Mr. Gray published, through the Boone and Crockett Club, a booklet entitled *Records of North American Big Game*. In 1939, after Gray's death, the Boone and Crockett Club, with the cooperation of the National Collection of Heads and Horns of the New York Zoological Society and The American Museum of Natural History, published a larger and revised list of records along with much other big game information under the title *North American Big Game*. It is to be anticipated that these published records will be

180

brought up to date periodically by one or more of the organizations concerned.

The American Museum of Natural History, New York City, regularly sends out forms to those requesting them who

A pair of locked whitetail heads.

believe they have trophies worthy of being listed. Some of these forms are illustrated on succeeding pages of this book for the information of interested sportsmen.

It is certainly desirable that some common grounds for judging excellence should be established. Europe has worked out a system but it does not appear to be well adapted to

American game species. Two or three systems have been developed in America. That most likely to find a permanent place is the one used by the compilers of the work mentioned above, which attempts to evaluate the factors of horn or antler length, number of regular or pattern points, circumference of horn or antler, total number of points, inside spread and symmetry between the two sides (with penalties for unsymmetrical features). Finally, a point number is given the trophy which determines its place on the list.

As an illustration: the score on the antlers of the whitetail deer is determined by adding the following measurements of both antlers together, plus the inside spread, and deducting such penalty points as may accrue for lack of symmetry. To the length of each main beam is added the length of the regular pattern points (up to the number of 8, if that many are present), the circumference of the antlers around the burr and at the smallest point between sets of regular points, beginning with the brow point but not including the measurement between the last upright point and the end of the main beam. The measurements thus obtained for the two sides are then added to the inside spread of the antlers, and from this are deducted any penalty points to determine the final score.

The penalty for non-symmetry is found by deducting the difference between the measurements of the two antlers plus the total lengths of all abnormal points (no points of less than 1 inch in length being counted). Thus symmetry is made a major consideration in determining the final point value of the trophy.

Attention may be called to the fact that whereas the main beam of the whitetail deer's antler is considered to be the one that curves forward, the main beam of the mule deer and blacktail is considered to be the one that rises to the greatest height. The forward branches are considered as

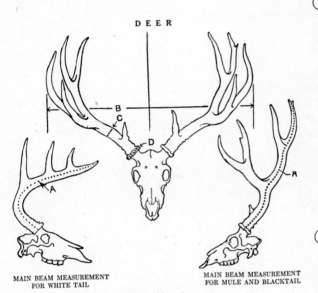

DEER

MAIN BEAM MEASUREMENT
FOR WHITE TAIL

MAIN BEAM MEASUREMENT
FOR MULE AND BLACKTAIL

Method of Measuring

All measurements **must** be made with a flexible steel tape.

A Length of outside curve: Measured along the main beam from the base of the burr to the tip of the most distant point on the main beam.

B Greatest spread: Measured between parallels and at right angles to the center line of the skull.

C Circumference: Measured midway between the basal snag and the first fork.

Points: No point shall be counted unless it extends at least one inch.

D Circumference of burr.

Remarks: State whether the trophy has any characteristics which depart from the normal for this species.

Records of North American
Big Game

IN CARE OF

AMERICAN MUSEUM OF NATURAL HISTORY

COLUMBUS AVENUE AND 77TH STREET

NEW YORK, N. Y.

B E A R

SPECIES ....

MEASUREMENTS

Greatest length overall **A** (Fig. 1)...

Width across the zygomatic arches **B** (Fig. 1)......................................

Weight of skull cleaned...

MEASUREMENTS

Length tip of nose to tip of tail **A** (Fig. 2)...

Length of tail **B** (Fig. 2)..   ....

Length of hind foot **C** (Fig. 2)...

Weight ....

Sex ....

Hide Length **BB** (Fig. 3)..

Width **AA** (Fig. 3)..

Exact locality where killed...

Date killed ....

By whom killed ....

Owner ....

Address ....

Remarks: ....

....

    We hereby certify that we have measured the above described trophy
on...193   , and that these measurements are
correct and made in accordance with the directions overleaf.

....

By ....

184

WAPITI

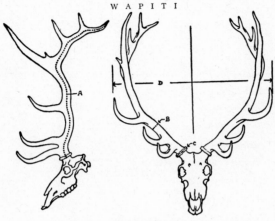

Method of Measuring

All measurements **must** be made with a steel tape.

A Length on outside curve: Measured along the main beam from the base of the burr to the tip of the most distant point on the main beam.

B Circumference midway between bez and trez.

C Circumference of burr.

D Greatest spread: Measured between perpendiculars at right angles to the center line of the skull.

Points on each side: No point shall be counted unless it protrudes at least two inches.

Remarks: State whether the trophy has any characteristics which depart from the normal for this species.

Please provide photographs showing front view and profile.

Record of North American
Big Game

IN CARE OF

AMERICAN MUSEUM OF NATURAL HISTORY
COLUMBUS AVENUE AND 77TH STREET
NEW YORK, N. Y.

D E E R

SPECIES..

MEASUREMENTS	RIGHT	LEFT
Length of outside curve **A**	....	....
Greatest spread **B**...................		
Circumference of main beam **C**	.,.......... ... .:.	
Number of points on antler	....	....
Circumference of burr **D**	....	....

Exact locality where killed..

Date killed...

By whom killed...

Owner... .

    Address..

Present location of trophy...

....

Remarks:...

....

We hereby certify that we have measured the above described trophy
on.................................194   , and that these measurements are
correct and made in accordance with the directions overleaf.

....

By ....

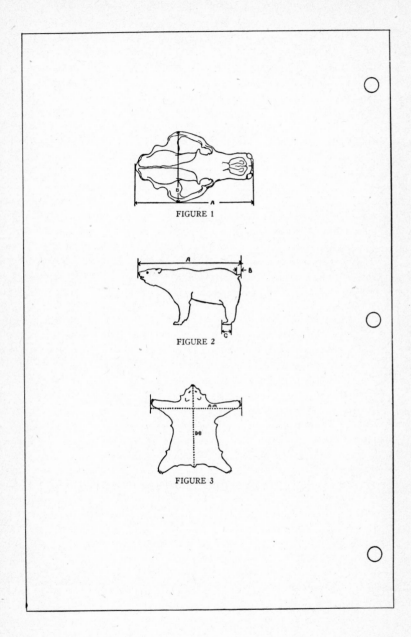

FIGURE 1

FIGURE 2

FIGURE 3

BEAR

Method of Measuring

All measurements **must** be made with a steel tape.

Skull measurements are made as indicated in figure 1. Length **A** and width **B** are taken between perpendiculars to the main axes of the skull.

Body measurements must be made in the field.

A Length tip of nose to tip of tail: The distance in a straight line from the tip of the nose to the tip of the tail not including the hair on the end of the tail. This must be measured between the perpendiculars after the head, neck and tail have been extended.

B Length of tail: Measured from the dorsal root of the tail to the fleshy tip of the tail, the hair on the end of the tail not being included. The easiest method of taking this measurement is to extend the tail upward at right angles from the back and measure from the rump, at the base of the tail, to the last bit of skin on the tail, the tail vertebrae to be kept perfectly straight.

C Length of hind foot: Measured from the edge of the heel to the tip of the claw on the longest toe, the foot extended and kept flat so that the curvature of the toes is straightened out.

Weight—actual weight.

Hide measurements are made by the Museum after the hide has been dried or tanned.

BB Length is the measurement from the tip of nose to the fleshy tip of tail.

AA Width is measured across the hide between the extreme ends of the claws of the forefeet. Length and width must be measured simultaneously or at least without moving the hide after the first measurement has been taken.

Remarks: State whether the trophy has any characteristics which depart from the normal for this species.

This record is naturally based on "owner's measurements" (except skull and hide measurements) and therefore we rely on the measurements by the Museum of the dried or tanned hide to check the measurements as made in the field.

secondary. The measurement and point system have been worked out individually for each species.

As this is written, a letter from the committee on record heads and horns states that the data received since the publication of *North American Big Game* have merely been filed but not evaluated "with any attempt to keep up a current list of records." With the exception of the Wyoming Moose, the table of record dimensions represents abbreviated compilations from the 1939 edition of *North American Big Game*. The moose listed was killed in Fremont County, Wyoming, by Arthur E. Chandler, of Casper, in 1944 and was reported to the author by Harold G. King, President, Natrona County (Wyoming) Game & Fish Association, with verified measurements by Jasper Hampton, Casper taxidermist.

The list of top-ranking heads and horns follows this page in tabulated form.

The largest bear skull on record came from the Alaska Peninsula and was 19 inches long and 11⅞ inches wide across the zygomatic arches. The bear with largest measurements on record for any killed outside Alaska was shot in Teton County, Wyoming; the skull measured 16¾ by 9¾ inches. The second largest, measuring 16 by 9¾ inches, was killed in Montana. Scientists find it impracticable to draw a line between where the Alaska browns leave off and the grizzlies begin.

The largest polar bear skull measured 18 by 10 inches; and the largest black bear skull on record was 14⅛ by 7¾ inches. The record black bear came from Alaska, and the second largest from Texas, with a skull measurement of 13¼ by 7¼ inches.

Species	Length of main beam R. L.	Greatest spread	Circumference of main beam R. L.	No. of points R. L.	Locality killed
Whitetail deer	30¾–27½	33½	4¾–4¾	12–14	Brit. Col.
Mule deer	34	37½	5	14–13	Wyoming
Blacktail deer	30½	23	5	3–3	California
Coues deer	20⅛–20⅛	18	4 –3¾	4–6	Arizona
Wapiti	64¾	49⅝	7⅝	7–7	Wyoming
Mountain caribou	65⅛–62¼	54½	7¾	23–15	Brit. Col.
Woodland caribou	50	44⅜	6⅛	19–18	Newfoundland
Barren ground caribou	67⅝	48½	7	15–23	Hudson Bay

	Greatest spread	Length of palm R. L.	Breadth of palm R. L.	No. of points R. L.	Locality killed
Canada moose	73	37¼	15⅝–20	14–15	Alberta
Alaska moose	77⅝	43 –45⅜	12¼	15–18	Kenai Peninsula
Wyoming moose	56⅝	39¾–40½	13⅜–14¼	13–15	Wyoming

	Length of curve		Circumference at base		Greatest spread	Locality killed
	R.	L.	R.	L.		
Bighorn sheep	49½	–48¼	16	–16⅛	23⅞	British Columbia
Stone sheep	50⅛	–51⅝	15⅛	–14¾	31	British Columbia
White sheep	47½	–47	13		26	Alaska
Desert sheep	44	–43½	17	–17	23⅞	Lower California
Rocky Mountain goat	12¼	–12½	5½		7 Sex, Female	British Columbia

	Length of curve	Circumference at base	Length of prong	Locality killed
Pronghorn antelope	20 5/16	7	R. 4½	Arizona

	Length of curve	Width at base	Greatest spread	Locality killed
Barren ground musk-ox	29	R. 8¼	28⅝	Barren Grounds
Greenland musk-ox	28½	6⅞	27	Ellesmere Land

Index

193